1612

THE *LANCASHIRE WITCH* TRIALS

a new guide by
CHRISTINE GOODIER

Dedication

This book is for Daniel and Charlie, with my love

Copyright © Christine Goodier 2011

Published by Palatine Books,
an imprint of Carnegie Publishing Ltd
Carnegie House,
Chatsworth Road,
Lancaster, LA1 4SL
www.carnegiepublishing.com

ISBN 978-1-874181-77-4

Designed and typeset by Carnegie Book Production

Printed and bound in the UK by Information Press, Oxford

Contents

Foreword

Lancaster Castle is on the threshold of change in 2011, but this does not diminish our ability to simultaneously commemorate the four-hundredth anniversary of one of the most infamous events in its long history.

Standing proudly above the town, guarding the citizens of Lancaster, the walls of the castle bear witness to many trials and executions, but none so fascinating as that of the Pendle witches in 1612. In the twenty-first century the facts may appear unbelievable and even fantastic. However, in this volume you are transported back to the early seventeenth century and asked to view the events from the perspective of social and religious attitudes at that time. Not to judge hastily, as it might appear others did at the time, but to consider and weigh up the evidence having regard to the prejudices and social uncertainty that enveloped England, which makes this story so extraordinary.

No one who has been involved with Lancaster Castle, whether as Constable, judge, prison guard, inmate or visitor, can fail to be enchanted by its history and dour beauty. Its walls are imbued with mysticism, its fabric steeped in history. Christine Goodier has been involved in Lancaster Castle for many years as a manager and friend of the Duchy of Lancaster. This volume seeks to open the door on a chapter in history about which much has been written – but with many preconceptions accepted as fact. Through diligent research and great insight she has invited us to see the facts in context and reach our own conclusions. No book can be definitive on such a dark and secretive part of this country's history, but I commend it to you as a thought provoking exposé which might inspire the curiosity of the reader to seek a more intimate knowledge – and even to visit the castle where the mystery unfolded and the grim conclusions were enacted.

Paul R Clarke CVO
Clerk of the Council
The Duchy of Lancaster
London

Introduction

In August 1612 a group of men and women from the Pendle area of Lancashire stood trial for witchcraft at the Summer Assize held in Lancaster Castle. Tried alongside them was a group of three women from Samlesbury, and two other women – one from Padiham near Burnley and the other from Windle, near St Helens. Collectively, they are known to history as the 'Lancashire witches'.

The trials took place at a time when the practice of witchcraft was no longer tolerated in England, so that those accused in 1612 found themselves facing the law at its most severe. Their supposed crimes, which once might have been viewed as acceptable to an extent, were now inextricably linked to malevolence and diabolism. This change in society's attitude to the witch figure had a lot to do with the religious upheavals taking place across Europe. Mankind's view of the supernatural, the unknown and even of the nature and worship of God Himself, was changing. And as many of the old beliefs and practices were swept away, what replaced them was less forgiving and much more certain of its own righteousness, and of the evil which could dwell in the human soul. The law as it stood in 1612 starkly reflected this view, and the people who prosecuted those accused of such crimes were more than ready to convict and condemn.

The defendants in the 1612 trials were not the first people to be accused of witchcraft, of course, and they would not be the last. Their 'crimes' were no more horrible than the crimes for which many others across the country stood trial, and yet they have taken their place among the most notorious of such cases. This is largely due to the publication of a pamphlet written on the orders of the presiding judges, and penned for them by the clerk of the court, Thomas Potts. *The Wonderfull Discoverie of Witches in the Countie of Lancaster* enjoyed a wide readership upon its publication in London in 1613, and it still has a kind of grim power today. Its contents are hard to read knowing as we do the outcome of the trials – that on 20 August 1612 ten people went to the gallows on the moors above Lancaster. Among their number were two men and a woman in her eighties. They had been condemned for laming, causing madness and for what was termed 'simple witchcraft'. In addition, sixteen unexplained deaths had been attributed to their malice.

The case seemingly exposed a network of evil, and a way of life that was too horrible for God-fearing Christians to contemplate. And yet, at the same time, it was something that many people were only too ready to believe existed. This belief was compounded by an apparent willingness on the part of the defendants to confess to the crimes of which they stood accused. Many of those involved in the Pendle case implicated themselves in events previously unknown to the authorities. Some, according to Potts, even went so far as to admit to having sold their souls to the Devil, perhaps not even realising that by so doing they were putting the noose around their own necks. A picture of fear and superstition, rivalry and hatred, seems to emerge from within the pages of sworn testimony taken by local JP and one-time High Sheriff of Lancashire, Roger Nowell. There was talk of cursing and of creating clay images to inflict pain and death. There were descriptions of 'familiar spirits' – the Devil in the shape of a dog or a boy or a man – that offered the accused worldly

power in return for their souls, and who sucked blood from secret places on their bodies. Claims and counter claims that came from within the ranks of the suspects themselves were to provide the most damning evidence possible for a court that seemed already to have decided to convict. It was a case that attracted great attention in its day and is a story that still has the power to capture the modern imagination.

My own interest in the case grew out of my seventeen-year association with Lancaster Castle. After graduating from Lancaster University in 1992 with a degree in

History, I was fortunate enough to be offered a job at the castle as a tour guide. It was wonderful to be able to talk about history for a living, and although I later became the manager of the Shire Hall section of the castle – a role which inevitably took me away from the coalface to a great extent – I never lost my love for the subject. I had taken a module on witchcraft as part of my degree and because it was the setting for the trials, the witches of 1612 will forever be part of Lancaster Castle's history. Over the years I have researched the cases, trying to work out to my own satisfaction exactly what might have been going on all those years ago. I found no easy answers to the abundance of questions thrown up by the cases, but one thing remained constant for me, and that was the simple fact that the accused were not fantasy figures but flesh and blood, men and women. It is this simple premise that underpins this book, and one of the main reasons I felt that it needed to be written.

Witchcraft is a nebulous term, one which is open to endless interpretation. What it means in any given society and at any given time is a key factor in how anyone accused of being a witch is treated. In some cultures the witch is revered and respected. In others they are vilified and outcast – even murdered – for their supposed powers. What is very clear is that by 1612 the perception of what constituted witchcraft had undergone a fairly recent and radical transformation. It was no longer ignored by the authorities, as it had once been, which was extremely bad news for the accused from Pendle, Windle, Padiham and Samlesbury, who stood trial in the grandeur of Lancaster Castle. Those sitting in judgement, along with those testifying against the defendants, were effectively projecting their own fears and beliefs onto the hapless people in the dock. They were finding what they expected to find in the tangle of hearsay and superstition that was the basis of the evidence; there was, truth be told, very little else.

This book is not intended to be an in-depth academic study of the subject of witchcraft, of which there are a good number already. In fact, the last few decades have witnessed an upsurge of serious interest in the topic as an historical phenomenon and this has resulted in several works, some of which have irrevocably altered the way we now approach the subject. Authors such as Keith Thomas, with his seminal work *Religion and the Decline of Magic*, have tried to make sense of old beliefs in the light of the rise of science and changes in the practice of religion itself. Other writers have carried out detailed studies of specific rural communities in order to unravel the social tensions that lay behind accusations of witchcraft, at the same time giving us a valuable insight into what life must have been like in such tight-knit communities over the course of the sixteenth and seventeenth centuries.

Nor do I intend to explore, more than is mentioned in Potts, the world of the spell, charm and curse. While such studies have their place I am much more interested in the historical and human aspects of the case. Whatever they had done, whatever they believed and whatever other people considered them to be, the accused were real people leading real lives, and I believe that fact can get lost and forgotten amid the myths and stereotypes that the word 'witch' inevitably drags along in its wake. What I want to do is to attempt to move past the many and varied re-tellings of the Lancashire witches' story and to return to the only primary source we have: Thomas Potts' account of the trials and the events that led up to them.

Potts is our only surviving written source, but obviously the contents of *The Wonderfull Discoverie* should be handled with a great deal of caution and a healthy dose of informed, albeit retrospective, scepticism. For one thing, it was written entirely with hindsight and with an absolute certainty of the guilt of the accused on the part of all who participated in their prosecution. It is also important to point out that although it tries very hard to be, it is not a verbatim transcript of the proceedings or a legal document. Tantalisingly, it seems that such a thing *did* exist because Potts alluded to it several times in his account of the trials, particularly during his account of the trial of James Device. It is also likely that part of the rationale behind the pamphlet would have been the desire to both justify the verdicts in Lancaster and to further the careers of those involved in prosecuting the case. The judge who presided at the trials, Sir Edward Bromley, was a key instigator in respect of the writing of the text, and he also revised and corrected it before it went to print. These factors surely have to be borne in mind as we come to look more deeply at the way the 'evidence' is presented within the pages of the pamphlet.

Having said all that, I have tried to look at the Lancashire witch trials with an empathetic regard for all concerned, and to put flesh on the bones of all those involved, not just the accused. How would any of us have fared had we been unfortunate enough to have had such an accusation levelled against us? How do you defend yourself against an idea? By the same token, what do you do if you sincerely believe that evil is running rampant among your friends and neighbours, and is threatening your own life and the lives of those you love? History asks as many questions as it answers, but the stark fact remains that ten people died in Lancaster in August 1612, executed by a court of law and under the terms of the law as it then stood, and that each of those people was either someone's wife, mother, grandmother, brother, sister or son.

All of which brings us back to Thomas Potts and his flawed but enthralling account. I hope that this book will allow the modern reader access to what can be a difficult text to read in its original form. I also hope that it will shed a little light on the wider world that lay beyond the confines of Pendle Hill, and on the religious, political, and social structures whose tentacles reached into the enclosed and isolated lives of the men and women who stood trial, plucking them from their simple, everyday existence and leaving them to face accusations that they cannot possibly have fully comprehended. Most of all – with the 400th anniversary of the trial approaching – I hope this book finally gives the voices of the defendants a fresh and fair hearing and allows readers to make up their own minds about what happened all those years ago.

My Thanks

To Michael Mullett and Robert Poole for reading the first draft of this book. I hope that I have taken on board their comments and I'm sure that the end result is better for their input. Any remaining errors and omissions are entirely my own.

To Paul Clarke CVO, Chief Executive and Clerk to the Council of the Duchy of Lancaster for agreeing to write the foreword.

To all my colleagues over the years at Lancaster Castle for their tireless hard work and determination in bringing a rich history and an amazing building to life for so many people.

I am very grateful to Ian Eastham for his wonderfully evocative photos of Pendle and also to Colin Penny and Paul Thompson for their photos of the castle.

Thanks also to David, Sarah, Alexander and Adrian.

And of course to Anna and everyone at Carnegie.

Why do I yield to that suggestion
Whose horrid image doth unfix my hair
And make my seated heart knock at my ribs,
Against the use of nature? Present fears
Are less than horrible imaginings.
My thought, whose murder yet is but fantastical,
Shakes so my single state of man that function
Is smother'd in surmise, and nothing is
But what is not.

William Shakespeare
Macbeth. Act 1 Scene 1

Part One: The Background

Pendle

Pendle is an area of Lancashire lying to the east of Clitheroe. It is bounded to the south by the River Calder, while Pendle Hill rises to the north west, a brooding presence looking down over a number of scattered villages and hamlets that have not changed greatly over the past four hundred years. The area is also known as the Forest of Pendle, which actually indicates that its primary use during the Middle Ages was as a chase or hunting ground rather than a forest *per se*. The land is only lightly dotted with clumps of trees that stand shaped by the force of the prevailing wind (perfect country for hunting), and the wide and often lowering sky looks down on a seemingly unchanging scene. Some of the land under Pendle was fertile, and some of the families that owned or rented such land and farmed there in the early years of the seventeenth century must have made a decent living. But a lot of the soil was too wet and too dense with peat for the widespread successful cultivation of crops, so the air was probably pierced only by the bleating of sheep as they grazed the fells and fields, or by the desolate cries of rooks and crows as they hovered in the sky, riding the wind.

Many of the villages mentioned in *The Wonderfull Discoverie* do, of course, still exist, and they are forever associated with the events of 1612: Downham and Newchurch-in-Pendle, Fence, Sabden, Barley and Blacko. It is easy to believe that this is still recognisably the same landscape over which the people caught up in the trials of four centuries ago would have trudged – begging, doing odd jobs, scraping a living in the only way they knew how.

Although the Pendle area is only some 30 miles to the south east of Lancaster and 12 miles west of Halifax, there is a sense of remoteness about the place, even today. At the time in question this isolation was magnified many times over. Lancashire was itself considered to be one of the most inaccessible counties in England, with poor roads that seemed to go literally nowhere. The main route to Scotland lay on the east of the county and the Lake District to the north was still viewed as a hostile and threatening landscape, a perception which was to linger into the eighteenth century. At the time in which the defendants, witnesses and victims lived, Lancashire was still – in many rural areas – wild and uninviting, and its inhabitants were perceived to be poor and ill-educated, and worse, suspect, by those who wielded the real power, so far away in London.

Part of this perception stemmed from events that took place eighty years before the trials in Lancaster, and were rooted, as was so much else during this period, in the religious turmoil of Tudor England. Pendle was part of the parish of Whalley, whose magnificent Cistercian abbey had dominated the area since 1296. During the Dissolution of the Monasteries during the reign of Henry VIII, the abbey suffered greatly and was stripped of its wealth and its place at the spiritual heart of the community. Further disaster followed when Whalley became involved in the Pilgrimage of Grace, a great and popular uprising in favour of the restoration of Catholicism that raged across the north of England in 1537, and which even, for a short time, threatened the power of the king. Henry quashed the rebellion and dealt with the rebels harshly after their defeat. The last abbot of Whalley, John Paslew, caught up in the rebellion, was tried and executed in Lancaster for high treason in 1537, and his remains were returned to the abbey to be hung in chains. After this time the area seems to have become both demoralised and devoid of strong spiritual guidance. This was compounded over the following decades by an apparent failure on the part of the burgeoning Anglican Church to fill the void left by the destruction of the abbey, leaving people, if the testimony given in 1612 is to be believed, to rely on their memories of old Catholic rites and teachings to fill their lives with meaning. These in turn seem to have become, on occasion, intermingled with elements of folklore. The result was a dangerous mixture indeed.

At the same time, the concept of charity, which was a central tenet of Catholic belief and teaching, was being eroded and altered. Where once it had been seen as a channel of grace for the giver to bestow alms and to care for the sick and the destitute – something that religious houses all across the country had been involved in to a greater or lesser extent – over the course of the Protestant Reformation it came to be regarded as primarily a financial burden. This burden was carried by local communities and was enough to transform the way in which the needy were viewed in society. Various laws were passed during the later sixteenth century that made caring for the poor the responsibility of their native parish, and there are even stories of pregnant women, destitute and homeless, being chased across parish boundaries so that their offspring would be the responsibility of whichever community they found themselves in at their birth. For many communities the financial burden was onerous, and, especially in hard times, begrudged. Gradually, those receiving handouts were judged by an increasingly stern moral yardstick. In the nineteenth century this was actually to be given a name, when paupers living 'on the parish' were divided into the 'deserving' and 'undeserving' poor, a concept that would usher in the rise of the dreaded workhouses. But it is not too hard to believe that this attitude may already have been current at the period we are concerned with, and it is notable that there were, among the accused of 1612, women with illegitimate children, and men who lived less than upright lives in the eyes of their neighbours. When times were hard, as they often were in the turbulent seventeenth century, this financial burden could translate into real hardship for those forced to pay for the upkeep of their less fortunate neighbours. It is not too difficult to see how this attitude might translate into superstitious anxiety when tragedy struck, and that this fear and superstition could then so easily mutate into the kind of accusations that were levelled against some of Pendle's poorest and most vulnerable inhabitants.

Far removed as it was from the centres of power, attached as it was to the old religion, and trapped as it was by its recent history, Lancashire became a sort of microcosm for the religious and political differences that were, some thirty years later, to plunge the entire country into civil war. So here was an area that was seen as unruly, troublesome and potentially dangerous. It was a place where, as the trials of August 1612 were to show, almost anything was believed to be possible. But of course, no event can be looked at in isolation, and there were many strands – religious, political and social – woven into the tapestry of the story of the Lancashire witches.

King James and Witchcraft

England at the start of the seventeenth century was a country still struggling to come to terms with the unprecedented changes that had taken place in its religious and social make-up. It was a Protestant nation; a country emerging into the Early-

Modern world and yet still tethered somewhat to its medieval past. The reign of Queen Elizabeth had been long and dazzling and she had been seen as *Gloriana* – the embodiment of the perfect queen. She was almost deified after her death, hindsight blurring her faults and failures so that she was revered as a woman who had guided the country through foreign threats and a goodly number of home-grown conspiracies. She had guided the country in religion too, attempting to steer a middle course through a plethora of diverse beliefs to a position of relative peace as well as financial prosperity. Never married, Elizabeth died in March 1603 and the throne passed to James VI of Scotland.

James was the son of Elizabeth's cousin, Mary, Queen of Scots, who for most of her adult life was seen by some to be Elizabeth's main rival for the English throne. A devout Catholic in a country fast becoming Calvinist, Mary had been driven from Scotland by her son's Protestant guardians in 1568, and replaced on the Scottish throne by James while he was still a small child. Mary fled to England and appealed to Elizabeth for help, but she was of course far too dangerous to be allowed to remain free and she was immediately imprisoned. Even as a prisoner, however, Mary quickly became the focus for many die-hard Catholics in England who were desperate to replace Elizabeth with a monarch of their own faith, one that would return England to the Catholic fold. In 1587, after the last in a very long series of plots in her name, Mary was executed at Fotheringhay Castle.

James, meanwhile, having been raised as a Protestant, was seen as a suitable successor when the time came for Elizabeth to name her heir. When news reached him in 1603 of Elizabeth's death, he hurried south at once and was welcomed into his new kingdom with a great deal of relief and goodwill. Here was a Protestant king with Tudor as well as Stuart blood, one who also had a young family and an heir. The future seemed assured. It was a situation that James was keen to maintain and build upon, and he lent an ear to the pleas of his subjects with laudable patience; there was even the apparent possibility of a rapprochement with the beleaguered English Catholic community, many of whom revered his mother as a martyr.

One of the first pieces of legislation passed under James was the 1604 Witchcraft Act. This Act imposed much harsher penalties for those convicted of witchcraft and also for anyone associating with, or assisting, them, and it reflected a change in attitude to the nature of the crime, one which emanated from the king himself. There was a personal element in James' attitude to witchcraft in that he was firmly convinced that he and his queen, Anne of Denmark, had been the intended victims of a plot to murder them by a group of supposed witches in Berwick in 1590. The Berwick case was the most notorious witch hunt in Scottish history. Before it ended over one hundred people had been implicated. Through the use of torture many of them confessed to the crime and were executed. James even went as a far as interviewing one of the suspects, Agnes Sampson, at Holyroodhouse in Edinburgh. After this time James studied the subject in depth and quickly became familiar with the 'continental' concepts of diabolic pacts, with so-called witches' Sabbats, and with the theory of an international conspiracy whose aim was the very overthrow of Christianity. It was an elite view resulting from theological debate and study, and this was reflected in the pages of the book James wrote on the subject in 1597. Entitled *Daemonologie,* it was a warning against the practice of witchcraft that drew on biblical and learned texts for its justification, and it differed greatly from the concept of witchcraft that had preceded it, which had been based on a belief in the power to do harm by magical means. This might be said to be the witchcraft of popular culture, which bore little relationship to the way that witchcraft started to be interpreted.

Daemonologie was an influential text but it has to be said that it did not go as far as other such volumes on the subject. The most famous and damaging of these was

the *Malleus Maleficarum* (Hammer of the Witches), an immensely influential text on the nature of witchcraft written in 1486 by two Dominicans, Heinrich Kramer and Jacob Sprenger. This was a book that in some respects actually helped to instigate the European witch hunt. Arriving at roughly the same time as the printing press, the *Malleus* ran into many editions and was widely read. It set forth the theory that the Devil used his evil to tempt the weak into his service, and it was Kramer's contention that this meant women in particular. He believed that women were the weaker sex not just physically but morally; they were more lustful and venal than men and thus were the perfect tools with which the Devil could ensnare men to do his will. The book documented in great and graphic detail how witches supposedly operated, their often physical relationship with the Devil and the many tools that they had at their disposal in order to spread the Devil's influence among mankind. The book was deeply misogynistic, full of hate, and without a shadow of a doubt was responsible for the deaths of hundreds of people across Europe during the fifteenth, sixteenth and seventeenth centuries.

Kramer claimed that he had Papal blessing to disseminate the contents of the book, but the truth was that it had been condemned by the Inquisition and that Kramer had been chastised for spreading such ideas. This did not stop him, and in fact he simply tried to add a spurious veneer of authority to his tract in order to carry its grisly message to an ever-widening audience, by using the well-respected Jacob Sprenger's name as co-author and by claiming that the contents had Sprenger's endorsement. It is probable that Sprenger was never actually connected with the book, although they have always been given as joint authors. The message of the book continued to spread and its twisted views were embraced as though they did, indeed, have official sanction. This was to be the case even after the Reformation, when Protestant, as well as Catholic, countries began sending so many of their citizens to the flames, convicted of the crimes that Kramer had included within the pages of his book, drawn in effect from the dark recesses of his own warped imagination.

King James would have been familiar with Kramer's book, and although *Daemonologie* was milder in tone than the *Malleus*, the themes put forward by Kramer undoubtedly coloured both the king's own text and his views on the subject. Although the term 'witch' had existed as a concept since Biblical times, the 'witch hunt' was something new. It was a phenomenon that spanned almost exactly 300 years – from the middle of the fifteenth century to the later decades of the eighteenth – and which affected most of the Christian world. Estimates of the number of people executed for witchcraft range from 500,000 to 9 million, with modern academic opinion tending toward the lower figure. In total, fewer than 500 people were executed for the crime in England (one of the lowest totals in Europe), although this is an appalling number of people to die for crimes we no longer believe even existed. Those caught up in the phenomenon included rich as well as poor, Protestant as well as Catholic, male as well as female. Outbreaks were sporadic in nature, and usually occurred in rural rather than urban areas. Typically, accusations could go back decades. And while women outnumbered men on a ratio of 3:1 in witchcraft prosecutions, it was far from being an entirely misogynistic crusade, despite the best efforts of people who upheld the views of Heinrich Kramer and his ilk, to make it so.

This tempering of the ferocity of the witch hunt in England might have been due in part to the fact that there was no history of an English Inquisition. The Inquisition was used on the continent by the Catholic Church as a means by which religious conformity could be policed. It was also a vehicle for the punishment of offenders should they be found to hold heretical beliefs, as well as an effective means of keeping a lid on the upsurge of Protestant belief in Catholic countries during the Reformation, but of course it was both feared and much hated. There was no such

body in England, and to a great extent people were still allowed to voice opinions as long as they fell within certain parameters (people were burned at the stake in England too, of course, for holding and voicing the wrong religious beliefs at the wrong time). One man who raised his head above the parapet to speak out against the belief in the existence of witchcraft was Reginald Scot. An MP from Kent born in 1538 and educated at Oxford, Scot set out his beliefs in a book of his own, *The Discoverie of Witchcraft*, in 1584, and despite the similarities in the titles there was nothing in Scot's book that would have pleased Thomas Potts at all. Scot held the view that witchcraft was a sham, a confidence trick, and that anyone pretending to practise the craft was a charlatan or else deluded. It was perhaps thanks to this freedom to speak and the courage of men like Scot to fly in the face of the prevailing beliefs of the time, that the witch hunt in England – bad as it was – never descended into the holocaust seen on the continent.

Also to be thanked (perhaps ironically) was the English legal system itself. In many European countries a suspect could not be convicted until they had confessed, and torture was used routinely to ensure that confess they did. In England, however, torture was not used in this way. There were degrees of ill treatment, it goes without saying, which were used to induce a confession without resorting to the hideous physical maltreatment to which a lot of the people executed across Europe were subjected. This included sleep deprivation or the practice of keeping someone in an uncomfortable position for hours on end, but torture *per se* was reserved in England for cases of suspected treason, or when a confession was required in order to speedily root out a conspiracy. This was the case, for example, with Guy Fawkes in 1605, a procedure which, as always, was carried out under the Royal Writ. Those accused at Lancaster in 1612, therefore – as was the case with any other defendant in a criminal trial – remained innocent until found guilty which shifted the burden of proof to their accusers and prosecutors. The fact remains that the burden was not a heavy one, and that testimony was largely based on hearsay coupled with vague memories of events that had, in some instances, taken place many years previously. This was often enough to secure a conviction because there was a common acceptance as to what a witch was, what they practised and what the outcomes of such practices were. But at least the defendants had their day in court, something that was denied to hundreds of similarly accused suspects elsewhere in Europe.

Because witchcraft was a rural phenomenon it is often assumed that those accused were somehow healers, using and dispensing herbal remedies. This does not seem to have been the case and I feel that it is important to state clearly at the outset that those who found themselves falling foul of the laws against witchcraft were never tried simply for administering herbal cures. Indeed, there would have been little need for this, as herbalism was commonplace and every housewife in the county with a plot of spare land at her disposal would have gained a working knowledge of herbal lore. It was an everyday necessity in an age when the medical profession was in its infancy. That is not to say that people desperate to find help for a sick loved one did not resort to those people considered to be in touch with a deeper, often darker, power to heal, and there were many such people in England at that time. Known as 'wise' or 'cunning' men and women, they were allowed to operate openly within their society and were not routinely associated with the practice of witchcraft unless some catastrophe befell their community or people had other reasons to start examining their actions. Knowledge of herbal lore, therefore, in and of itself was never the sole cause for an accusation. It had to be associated with other things, such as the casting of spells or the use of an illegally obtained object or substance – often human in origin such as blood or bones – for this knowledge to be branded as witchcraft. Midwives, who might be expected to rank highly on any list of suspects because of their close association with the mysteries of birth and the high death rate among the newborn and of women in childbirth, were not routinely accused either. With a one-in-three chance of a woman dying in childbirth, the services of midwives were actually highly valued in a time before an exclusively male medical profession emerged and slammed its door in such women's faces. It would later emerge that Puerperal Fever, the cause of many of these tragic deaths, was a result of bad hygiene, but, perhaps surprisingly, cases of such deaths being attributed to witchcraft are virtually non-existent, at least in England. Indeed the search of a suspect's body for the tell-tale 'witch marks' that were believed to exist was often carried out by such women at the behest of the authorities.

Witchcraft and History

There has been a great reassessment of seventeenth-century history in recent years, including a growing interest in the subject of witchcraft. It is a subject fraught with difficulties for the modern historian, of course, which is not because there is a dearth of information but because there is so much. Looking at the evidence of prosecutions it is hard to think oneself back into a mindset and an era when clearly outrageous claims could find their way into the courts of England and be given such credence.

The accused, as we have seen, were more often women than men and they were usually widows or spinsters living on the edges of their societies. Rivalries and tensions exist in all close communities and it was common for discontent and suspicion to rumble on for a long period of time before some unexpected or unexplained event tipped the balance and an accusation of witchcraft was made. The preponderance of accusations in rural areas with small communities highlights the fact that the supposed victim of a curse or malicious act almost always knew the accused. Accusations hardly ever occurred in the larger centres of population, most probably because people simply did not know their neighbours in the same intimate fashion and were increasingly distanced from the rhythm of the natural world. In some cases it seems that a sort of hysteria would convince people (even those not personally afflicted by whatever sudden death or illness was being called into question) of the 'witch's' guilt, so that very quickly the accused would be viewed with suspicion by the community as a whole. Many defendants in witch trials found themselves suddenly friendless, any past acts of kindness they might have performed (curing a sick cow, taking a curse off curdled milk) soon forgotten as the act quickly came to be regarded as yet more proof of their perceived evil nature.

The Lancashire case was the first witch trial in English history to contain 'evidence' that related to the more 'continental' aspects of witchcraft – the very witchcraft to be found described within the pages of the *Malleus* and, more significantly, *Daemonologie*. Familiar spirits, Sabbats and pacts with the Devil, for instance, were all aspects of witchcraft that King James detailed in his treatise on the subject, and as we have seen Potts made reference to *Daemonologie* with regard to the proceedings in Lancaster. However, while it has been argued that far from being a 'witch-hunter's reference book' *Daemonologie* was in fact an attempt to curb the excesses of witch hunts, it does seem to have been used as the defining source of reference for those prosecuting the cases in Lancaster in 1612. While some modern observers have decided that Potts' references to King James' book stemmed from the need to justify the convictions in Lancaster in the face of a growing scepticism within the English elite (and even on the part of the king himself), there would seem to be little point in twisting the evidence to fit a concept of witchcraft in which the king had ceased to believe. And it has to be said that the nature of witchcraft accusations and trials did not alter over the remainder of the reign. Significantly, neither did the way in which they were dealt with by the courts.

Catholic Lancashire

There had been a time, not that long before the period in which the Lancaster trials took place, when England and indeed most of mainland Europe had been Catholic. King Henry VIII, although never a Protestant himself, had, by the time of his death in 1547, destroyed the infrastructure of the Catholic Church in England and, denying the power of the Pope, set himself up as head of the new English church. The Reformation proper in England progressed during the short reign of his only surviving son, Edward VI, but on Edward's death in 1553 the throne passed to Henry's daughter, Mary. She was the child of Henry's first marriage, to Catherine of Aragon, and had been raised a devout Catholic. She clearly saw it as her duty to return England to Catholicism. This resulted in the burnings and persecution of Protestants and revolted those of the new religion, leaving a legacy of hatred for, and fear of, those who remained Catholic after Mary was dead. This fear had been intensified and reinforced by the publication of John Foxe's *Book of Martyrs* in 1563, a book which contained fearful images and countless tales of atrocities committed against Protestants in the name of religion. The woodcuts in the *Book of Martyrs* bear a stylistic similarity to those in the *Malleus*, and for anyone encountering them – especially the illiterate – these illustrations must have been terrifying. The book was widely disseminated in churches and nearly every churchgoer (that is almost the entire population) would have seen the book at some time. It was a grisly warning of what man was capable of and a reinforcement of the belief that any amount of evil could be at large, hidden beneath a veneer of normality, just waiting to pounce and destroy.

Lancashire was, of course, officially part of the Anglican Communion, but at the same time much of it continued to be the heartland of the old religion, with some areas of the county remaining, albeit clandestinely, Roman Catholic. This situation was to some extent exacerbated by the failures of the Anglican Church itself, as we have seen with the Church's failure to fill the void left by the Dissolution of Whalley Abbey. The parish livings within the county tended to be poor, with little hope of advancement for the men assigned to them, and this resulted in a clergy that was more often than not inept and uninterested in ministering to its flock. Where Protestantism thrived in Lancashire it tended to be of a more radical nature, with Calvinism at its core. This was a doctrine that espoused the concept of Predestination:

the belief that a soul was either saved or damned from birth, and that nothing a person did in this life could change the soul's predetermined fate. This was to lay the foundation for the so-called 'Protestant work ethic', and the belief that the sign of a person's righteousness was earthly success. Conversely, if someone failed, was poor or deformed or lazy, then this was an outward sign of their ultimate damnation. And if God had given up on a soul, what right had man to try to save it? It was a world view that allowed little room for tolerance at this time, either towards the 'undeserving' poor, as they were later termed, or towards other Protestants. It certainly allowed for little understanding when it came to Catholicism.

It is important to state here that the people accused in 1612 were Christian both in their upbringing and heritage. For a time in the early years of the twentieth century, writers such as Margaret Murray believed in the existence of a European cult of witchcraft that stretched back into the Celtic Twilight, one which had continued from then up to the present day. The existence of such an unbroken line of belief and practice was seized upon by people eager to claim historical validity for their own burgeoning beliefs, and it was not until the end of the century that Murray's work was finally shown to have been fatally flawed. Whatever the state of the modern religion of Wicca (the word from which 'witch' is derived), it is fair to say that it no longer claims this link, and that it certainly has no wish to be associated with the darker side of witchcraft as portrayed in trials such as those that took place in Lancaster four hundred years ago. And just as the accused were not simply wise-women selling herbal remedies, so neither were they adherents of Wicca – a term and a concept they would never have encountered or understood. Their background was firmly rooted in Catholicism and it was to be their use of Catholic language within their supposed spells and incantations that was to be most held against them, for adherence to the old religion was, by 1612, a very dangerous thing in and of itself.

For decades English Catholics had been viewed with suspicion, but after the excommunication of Queen Elizabeth I by the Pope in 1570, Catholics also began to be seen as a 'fifth column'. Although most of the Catholic community was loyal to the throne, the Gunpowder Plot of 1605 had had a negative impact on the position of Catholic families, destroying, at a stroke, the goodwill James I had held for them on his accession. There was an extensive underground network of Catholics in Lancashire. Many gentry families belonged in name only to the Church of England, attending Anglican services on Sundays to avoid the fines and imprisonment imposed upon those who failed to do so. These people were known as Church Papists and were largely tolerated by the authorities, unlike their more militant, open co-religionists who defied the law entirely. Known as Recusants, they refused to attend Anglican services and suffered for their faith, many spending long terms imprisoned and facing financial ruin. Because they still practised their true religion in secret, Catholic priests often worked in Lancashire, baptising infants, sanctifying marriages, saying mass and hearing confession, and saying prayers for the dead and the dying. They ran terrible risks by so doing. If they were apprehended they were charged with treason under Elizabethan legislation, and the courts were more than ready to convict such men, imposing the most horrendous penalties upon them, including execution by hanging, drawing and quartering.

On a more mundane level, however, and for the majority of ordinary people who conformed to the Anglican Church, the most obvious effect of the 'new' religion was a shift away from the rituals and the rhythm of their lives that had been afforded them by the Catholic Church. Graves were no longer sprinkled with salt to ward off evil, for example. Confession was gone too, as was Extreme Unction (last rites). As the Reformation deepened, not only were these rites considered redundant, they were actively decried as demonic and the Catholic Church itself equated with the work of the Devil. Even if it registered only at a subconscious level, there must have been a feeling of vulnerability at this time of transition. It is interesting to note the use of 'dog-latin' in some of the charms attributed to suspects in the 1612 cases, and that this throw-back to the old ways actually helped convince anyone who still needed convincing of the defendants' guilt. The other case of suspected witchcraft tried at the 1612 assize involved suspected witches from Samlesbury, and hinged upon the discovery of a Catholic plot against them. The 'evidence' of a Catholic conspiracy was enough to gain acquittals for all concerned even though the other evidence against the accused seemed, on the face it, to be just as damning as that brought against the defendants from Pendle.

There was also a clear connection between the authorities' desires to suppress and discredit the Catholic community and the choice made of a sponsor for *The Wonderfull Discoverie*. As was common at this time, a nobleman was sought to back the work and add his name to it to indicate his agreement with the contents. Interestingly, Potts, seeking patronage for his pamphlet, chose none other than Thomas, Lord Knyvet. Sir Thomas was Baron of Escrick in Yorkshire and had been appointed to the Privy Council under King James in 1607. Cambridge educated and related by marriage to members of the nobility, it was a shrewd choice as Sir Thomas was a fierce opponent of Catholicism and a man who had been instrumental in uncovering the 1605 Gunpowder Plot. Knyvet had been the officer charged with checking the cellars below Parliament on the night before the state opening in 1605, where he had, of course, discovered and arrested Guy Fawkes. After this event Knyvet's fortunes flourished and he became something of a favourite of the king.

By 1612, however, his star was declining, and he was trying hard to maintain the king's favour by reminding him, wherever possible, of the part he had played in saving James from Catholic conspiracy. He was, therefore, a good target for Potts and the judges, and it may well be that Knyvet agreed to endorse the contents of Potts' book as part of his continued efforts to regain royal favour. Perhaps this was also the reason behind the inclusion, within the *Wonderfull Discoverie*, of a quite bizarre claim: a supposed plot to blow up Lancaster Castle by the remaining 'witches' in an attempt to free their fellows incarcerated there. Of all the testimonies obtained from the suspects in the 1612 case this seems the most questionable. If such a plot was ever actually formulated then the plan was surely never going to succeed. Why any of the defendants would admit to this – if they ever actually did – is an interesting question, but it certainly made a perfect vehicle for anyone intent upon proving that, beneath the surface of everyday life in Lancashire, there lurked conspiracy, danger and deceit. Here was not only a coven of dangerous witches, but also another gunpowder plot, one moreover, against a royal castle: the title Duke of Lancaster, which had passed to James at his accession, is an hereditary honour passed down in turn to each reigning monarch, and ownership of Lancaster Castle has remained with the monarch since 1399, when the third duke, Henry Bolingbroke, became king as Henry IV. This plot had been foiled, then, not only by the diligence of the king's servants in Lancashire, but, by association, of Thomas Knyvet. This was fortuitous indeed and Knyvet must have been delighted to have been part of it, if only from a distance.

As with everything in Potts' book there was no corroborating evidence, no voice to deny that such a plot ever existed, no one to question the means by which a group of poverty-stricken and uneducated labourers and elderly women could have hoped to achieve this end, and blow up the vast fortress that was Lancaster Castle. They had all either died or fled the county by the time the book went to print and who was there left to raise a questioning voice or even care enough to cast doubts on what was appearing in print in London? But the inclusion of this plot throws light on what was going on in the minds of the authors for us today, and makes its inclusion vitally important for that reason alone.

Part Two: The Pendle Witches

Pendle: because of its associations with the trials of 1612, the name conjures up a hundred images: windswept and desolate fells, tiny hamlets with run-down farms struggling to survive in the more remote backwaters of rural Lancashire. It hints of the darkness of long winter evenings in remote cottages, with the wind rattling in the eaves and setting the candles flickering. The light from the fireplace conjures strange and shifting shapes along the walls and over the ceilings, and the old tell stories of ghosts and boggarts and witches to the wide-eyed young. Etched against stormy clouds and driving rain, images abound of bent and crooked humanity, half-crazed with delusions of illicit power, trudging the lanes, haunting the doorsteps of uneasy neighbours, relying on their reputations to keep them from starvation – their 'victims' too frightened of an unsure future to risk refusal of whatever boon they are asked for from the sinister shadow that appears, with such predictable regularity, at their door.

The term 'witch' itself also conjures up images of countless evil crones from all our childhoods. From Sleeping Beauty to Hansel and Gretel, the murderous woman appears, clothing her true nature in a garb of grand, or step-motherly sweetness, before revealing the horror beneath. And then there are the props without which any stereotype is incomplete – a broomstick, a pointy hat, a cauldron and a black cat. Not even Shakespeare was immune: his weird sisters concoct potions from unspeakable ingredients and chant as they foresee Macbeth's dark future in their malevolent blind eyes. And of course Shakespeare was not writing solely for the king or an elite audience when he penned the 'Scottish play' in 1606–7. He would have known that his witches would be instantly recognisable to the meanest of the groundlings that frequented the theatre. Shakespeare had his witches conjure storms, echoing perhaps the events that led up to the Berwick case. They foresee the future, consort with demons, use murder to procure the ingredients for their potions. This was already a powerful image of what witchcraft was capable of, and it was firmly embedded in the popular imagination several years before the Lancashire case.

But when we come to look at the truth behind the fantasy – as inevitably we must – to search for the reality behind the stereotype, what do we find? As with the historical reality that lies behind any myth or legend, what we find is both less than we were expecting and more. Less of the fantastic and more of the mundane; less of the fairy story and more of the universal reality of what it means to be human. The people accused in 1612 were just that: human. Men and women of flesh and blood, people of their time, people struggling to eke out a living in the only way they could. The only difference was that their actions were to be the subject of fierce and condemnatory scrutiny, their very existence was to be twisted to fit them for a fate none of them could have foreseen, and for which none of them could possibly have been prepared.

At a time when infant mortality was high and the average life expectancy was a little over forty, it is perhaps small wonder that unexplained and sudden death was often attributed to witchcraft. These fears and suspicions often festered for long periods of time and we find accusations in the Pendle case in particular, going back many years. In many respects people accused of witchcraft were society's scapegoats, a reason for the random ills that afflicted God-fearing and hard-working men and women. After all, they could not blame God, so who did that leave but the Devil and his instrument, the witch. The fact that those accused were poor or old or deformed only added to the perception of them as somehow 'other', leaving them even more marginalised and therefore even more threatening – a sort of self-fulfilling prophecy.

The suspects from Pendle were drawn from a small number of local families. At the head of each of the two families at the centre of the story was a matriarch: Elizabeth Southern who was known as Old Demdike, and Anne Whittle, known as Old Chattox. The families lived within a short distance of each other and their paths must have crossed on a regular basis. It seems that Elizabeth Southern was frail, blind and lame. When out begging she regularly leant on the arm of one of her grandchildren, who were the offspring of her daughter Elizabeth Device, whose husband John died in 1601. Elizabeth had three children – a son James and two daughters, Alizon and Jennet, the latter of whom must have been illegitimate if her age in 1612, given as nine, is to be believed. Southern had an illegitimate child as well – a son, Christopher Howgate – of whom very little is known beyond the fact that he and his wife fled the county soon after the first arrests in March 1612. Anne Whittle was also an old woman by the time the trials started, possibly in her eighties. She had two daughters – Anne, and Elizabeth, known as Bessie. Anne was the wife of Thomas Redfearne and had one daughter, Mary. It seems that they rented a cottage belonging to the Nutter family of Greenhead – with whom they seem to have had an uneasy, not to say acrimonious and precarious, relationship – while Old Demdike lived at Malkin Tower.

The two women must have known each other all their lives. They had probably been girls together, married and raised families and then been widowed, before beginning the long slow descent into old age, frailty and poverty. They were not friends in any sense of the word at the time of the accusations and trials. In fact, theirs had been a relationship, no matter how it had begun, ultimately based on mutual distrust bordering on hatred. They were also rivals, scraping by on reputations they had earned over the years as women not to cross, women who knew more than was healthy about things that ordinary, decent people, should not know. They were also women without men, and it is a strange concept to the modern mind, but this, by itself, would have been cause for some suspicion and concern at the beginning of the seventeenth century, when women were still considered to be property. With no father or husband, a woman was deemed to be 'masterless' and could easily have been viewed with suspicion by her neighbours and the authorities. Such a woman was also likely to be a financial drain on the community, and with no man to earn a living, would inevitably have to rely on the generosity of others in order to survive. Of course, there was a large number of women in this position throughout all ranks of society, and most were never suspected of wrong-doing. But couple this with poverty and 'deviant' behaviour (drunkenness, making a nuisance of themselves or bearing many illegitimate children for example) and you have a picture of many of the women cited in witch trials. Add to the mix a reputation for divination, spell-casting, healing or the perceived ability to cause harm if slighted, and you have the perfect ingredients for the type of accusations that flourished throughout England at this time.

The above model fits the majority of those caught up in the Pendle case, most of those involved having to survive by begging or by doing odd jobs for their better-off neighbours – maybe even by offering their supposed supernatural services in times of need. For people with few means of survival this low-level extortion, with its attendant threat of malevolence hanging over anyone who slighted them, got them

by. And they did hold grudges: Old Chattox was paid an annual 'tythe' by John Device, Old Demdike's son-in-law – who clearly believed in her power to do harm – on the understanding that she would leave him alone. The first time he refused to pay up he fell ill, and died proclaiming himself the victim of Chattox's malice. Such an incident can only have exacerbated an already long-running enmity between the two families. John's two older children, James and Alizon, must have known of the circumstances of their father's death from their mother and grandmother, and this may well have made it easier for them to co-operate with the authorities when the time came for them to be questioned. It also seems to be the case that they themselves believed that they possessed magical powers, and witchcraft had become a sort of family business for both families.

Of the other accused we know much less; Alice Nutter was most probably a yeoman farmer's wife who either rented the house at Roughlee or a cottage on the estate, while Katherine Hewitt lived with her husband in Colne, and prior to the evidence given against her by James Device and others, she had 'lived in the world free from suspicion', according to Potts. Alice Grey was also from Colne and she was listed by Potts as one of the defendants in the Pendle case. She then seems to become mixed up in his mind with the defendants from Samlesbury, and his final mention of her is that she was acquitted. The Bulcocks are shadowy figures. We know that they were mother and son and that Jane was a widow from Moss End. Some versions of *The Wonderfull Discoverie* list them as being acquitted, which has been the cause of confusion in the past, as they were actually convicted and executed. Margaret Pearson was probably, to put it bluntly, Nicholas Bannister's attempt to be involved in the case. A fellow magistrate of Roger Nowell, he must have been feeling a little left out of the great events uncovered by his colleague, and Pearson, who came from Padiham, was a fortuitous addition to the trials as far as he was concerned. She had faced two trials for witchcraft prior to this one – both times being acquitted – and Bannister must have seen her as an ideal way into the trials, when he arrested her on some of the most ridiculous and yet alarming evidence surely ever heard in an English court of law. Isobel Roby was the only one of the accused not to be known to any of the other defendants; she was committed for trial by Lord Gerrard, hereditary lord of the manor of Windle, near St Helens.

The Beginning — Alizon Device meets John Law

The Wonderfull Discoverie is an endlessly confusing text. It moves from the testimony taken at the time of the first arrests to the evidence given at the trials, and back again, so that a chronology is difficult to grasp on first reading. In this section I hope to simplify and straighten things out somewhat, and to begin at the beginning – with the seemingly innocuous event of a chance meeting one spring day between Alizon Device and John Law, a peddler from Halifax. I have also confined myself only to the evidence that appears in *The Wonderfull Discoverie.*

The story of the 1612 witchcraft case (although its roots stretched back many years) had its beginning following an incident that occurred on 18 March on the road to Colne. According to sworn testimony given at Read Hall before Roger Nowell after the event, Old Demdike's granddaughter Alizon Device was out begging. She met the peddler, John Law, and asked him for some pins from his sack, a request he refused. Peddlers at this time were often the lifeblood of rural communities. They brought with them not just the everyday necessities of life such as pots and pans but also the occasional luxury in the shape of dyed cottons or lengths of ribbon. They were also a valued link with outside world, bringing news and gossip along with their wares. Quite often peddlers such as John Law went from village to village on foot, which meant that they were physically fit. John's age was not mentioned in Potts' account but he had a grown son so was probably at least in his forties at the time of his encounter with Alizon.

Having refused Alizon her pins, John set off down the road. Alizon's familiar spirit apparently then appeared to her in the shape of a dog, and asked her if he could punish Law for his refusal of her pleas. Alizon, new to the art – if we are to give credence to what she told Nowell – and reluctant to have anything to do with the 'family business', supposedly asked the dog what could be done and the dog told her he could lame Law, to which course of action Alizon supposedly agreed. To Alizon's shock, the curse seemed to take immediate effect and John Law fell to the ground, paralysed down one side and unable to speak. These symptoms incline us to believe that John had suffered a stroke, but he believed, she believed and everyone else who heard the tale believed, that Alizon had cursed him.

John was taken to a nearby alehouse where he lay insensible for some time. Alizon carried on begging in and around Trawden, but John was later to testify that he was constantly plagued, all through those early days of his illness, by the sight of her, and the image of the 'big black dog' that he was convinced had harmed him. John's son, Abraham, was called over from Halifax to his sick father's bedside, and this was the moment when events began to get out of hand. John had recovered the power of speech by the time Abraham arrived, and he told his son that Alizon had bewitched him. Abraham had the girl brought to his father's bedside. She immediately confessed to the crime, then fell to her knees and begged his forgiveness. It actually seems that this was enough to satisfy John, who, perhaps alone among the people associated with this trial, emerged as a person of integrity and compassion. He must have been a strong, capable man, in the best of health to have done the work he did, and his affliction had reduced him to a pitiable state, one that was later to move the court to charity when he appeared at Alizon's trial. But if John was ready to forgive Alizon (or maybe was so frightened of her that perhaps he just wanted no more to do with her) his son most certainly was not. Abraham took the matter to Roger Nowell, the JP for the area.

Questioning at Read Hall — Enter Roger Nowell

It seems likely that, as a local magistrate, Roger Nowell would have already had some knowledge of the families he now started to question. He would already have been under orders from London to maintain a close watch on 'suspect' families in the area under his jurisdiction – mainly so that Recusant Catholics could be identified, but this could well have included any that might be the potential cause of unrest. If Old Demdike was the powerful witch that she herself and others seem to have believed her to be, then her reputation must have brought her to his attention, even if there are no records of any formal contact between them.

Roger Nowell had other, more personal, interests in the subject of witchcraft. He was, of course, socially as well as professionally well connected in the area, with family ties stretching throughout Lancashire and beyond. Raised a Protestant with family members who had been forced to flee England during the Marian persecutions, he also had knowledge of a particularly dark, not to say notorious, episode, which had involved members of his family at first hand. In 1595 Roger's nephew Nicholas Starkie, his wife Anne and their two young children were living at Cleworth near Leigh. For no apparent reason the children, a boy and a girl both under the age of twelve, began to suffer strange bouts of illness, which manifested itself in fits and convulsions. The children's health began to decline and although Starkie spent a considerable amount of money in an attempt to obtain a cure, he was unsuccessful. At their wits' end, Starkie and his wife eventually came to the conclusion that the children had been possessed.

A well-known local wise-man, Edmund Hartley, was engaged to cure the children. He was paid to live with the family and was, if later evidence is to be believed, something of a sexual predator. But he had some success and the children's health began to improve, so Starkie and his wife seem to have been happy to turn a blind eye to the means Hartley was supposed to have used in obtaining a cure, which included 'Popish' charms. Hartley then demanded more money from the family and when it was not forthcoming the illness returned and this time affected not just the children but the entire household. The servants and the female members of the household accused Hartley of 'bewitching them with his kisses' and other sexual advances, and the entire house seems to have been the scene of hysteria in varying degrees for a period of many months. Hartley was finally arrested and taken to Lancaster for trial. Dubious evidence was used against him and ultimately he was convicted and executed for witchcraft. Despite this the possessions continued and in desperation the Starkies turned for help to no less a person than John Dee, who was arguably the most famous astrologer, mystic and alchemist of his day. On his advice an exorcism was performed by two Puritan divines and this seemed to finally rid the family of its troubles. Sadly for the Starkies things didn't end there, because shortly after this the men who had conducted the exorcism were accused of chicanery. In their own defence they published accounts of their many supposed successes that of course now included the Starkie case. By 1612 the family had moved to Huntroyd and Roger Nowell would, no doubt, have discussed the accusations against the Pendle accused with them. There are certainly echoes of the Hartley case in the evidence given during the trials of 1612, especially in the use of Catholic language contained in charms. There can be little doubt that Nowells' knowledge of what members of his own family had suffered through would have been at the forefront of his mind as he dug deeper into the case that was now unfolding about him.

Nowell's decision to bring Alizon in for questioning was a swift one, and whether or not she realised the full implications of what she was saying when she appeared before him at Read Hall, it seems that she readily confessed to Nowell to having lamed John Law. Nor did she stop there; she went on to tell Nowell of her familiar spirit and how he had sucked her blood, and about her grandmother's long past as a witch. Mixed in with tales of turning milk sour and bewitching cows (both classic instances of what was known as *maleficium*) was the story of how Demdike had bewitched the daughter of Richard Baldwin to death after Baldwin had quarrelled with her. Demdike had also brought about the death, according to Alizon, of John Moore's son by making a clay image of the boy and slowly crumbling it, while Hugh Moore had died after accusing Demdike of bewitching his cattle.

These were devastating claims. Alizon had already confessed to crimes punishable by death, and now she was hinting at a network of evil that spread throughout the entire area. It was not a situation that Nowell could, or would, allow to continue, and he began to question those implicated by Alizon's admissions. Most importantly, this included Demdike herself. She was questioned by Nowell at Fence on 2 April and Potts included much of what was said at this meeting in his pamphlet, although Demdike herself never stood trial: sometime between April and August 1612, she was to die in the dungeon below the Well Tower in Lancaster Castle, a place more commonly known today as the Witches' Tower.

Old Demdike

By whatever means the statements taken during the days of early spring 1612 were obtained, there is no doubt that what emerged was an account of epic proportions. What Nowell and the others heard that April was astounding, and although Thomas Potts never actually set eyes on Demdike, he was more than willing to give a damning description of her, no doubt influenced by what he had heard of the woman from

Nowell and his associates. She was, according to Potts, a 'damnable and malicious witch … a sinke of villanie and mischiefe'. He justified the inclusion of Demdike's reported confessions as being vital to the entire saga of witchcraft in Pendle Forest throughout the last decades of the sixteenth and early years of the seventeenth century, and stated that all that had happened there had its origin with her.

> Shee was a very old woman, about the age of four-score yeares, and had been a witch for fiftie yeares. Shee dwelt in the Forrest of Pendle, a vaste place, fitte for her profession: what she committed in her time, no man knowes. Thus lived she securely for many yeares, brought up her owne children, instructed her Graund-children, and tooke great care and paines to bring them up as witches. Shee was a general agent of the Devill in all these partes: no man escaped her, or her Furies, that ever gave them any occasion of offence, or denyed them any thing they stood in neede of, no man neare them, was secure or free from danger.

Potts then recounted the origin of Demdike's career as a witch, the point at which the Devil first approached her and offered her whatever her heart desired if she would give him, in return, her soul. It was a story that was repeated (with only subtle differences) several times throughout the trial, and it is worthy of reproduction here in full:

> Twenty yeares past, as shee was coming homeward from begging, there met her this Examinate near unto a Stonepit in Gouldshey, in the sayd Forrest of Pendle, a Spirit or Devill in the shape of a Boy, the one halfe of his Coate blacke, and the other browne, who bade this Examinate stay, saying to her, that if she would give him her Soule, she shoulde have any thing that she would request. Whereupon this Examinate demaunded his name? and the Spirit answered, his name was Tibb: and so this Examinate in hope of such gaine as was promised by the sayd Devill or Tibb, was contented to give her

Soule to the said Spirit: and for the space of five or sixe yeares next aftere, the sayed Spirit or Devill appeared at sundry times unto her this Examinate about Day-lighte Gate, always bidding her stay, and asking her this Examinate what she would have or doe? To whom this Examinate replyed, Nay nothing: for she this Examinate said she wanted nothing yet. And so about the end of sixe yeares, upon a Sabbath day in the morning, this Examinate having a little child upon her knee, and she being in a slumber, the sayd Spirit appeared unto her in the likeness of a browne dogge, forcing himself onto her knee, to get blood under her left Arme: and she being without any apparrell saving her Smocke, the said Devill did get blood under her left Arme. And this Examinate awakening, sayd, Jesus save my childe; but had no power, nor could not saye, Jesus save herself; whereupon the Browne Dogge vanished out of this Examinates sight; after which this Examinate was almost starke madd for the space of eight weekes.

As Alizon had already, Demdike now also seemingly confessed to a capital crime, and then went on to list others. On one occasion, led by Alizon due to her blindness and infirmity, Demdike said that they had been threatened by Richard Baldwin with the words, 'Get out of my grounde Whores and Witches, I will burne the one of you and hang the other'. Tibb, the dog familiar, then appeared and offered to exact revenge on their behalf, the result of which was, as we have seen, supposedly the death of Baldwin's daughter.

Demdike also described a method of taking someone's life by the use of a 'picture' of clay made in their image, which could then be used to inflict pain or even death on the person it represented. According to Demdike, Old Chattox was an expert practitioner of this particular art. She told Nowell how she had once come upon Chattox, along with her daughter Anne Redfearne, fashioning clay images of Robert Nutter and other members of his family, in the company of Tibb, this time in the shape of a black cat. Demdike had declined to assist them, but within days Nutter was dead.

Old Chattox

Anne Whittle was the next to be questioned, and what she told Nowell and his associates must have only played into his hands. Here again was another tale of demonic pacts, of familiar spirits (in Chattox's case a young man she named 'Fancie') and of an evil so appalling as to be unbearable for a 'very religious, honest gentleman', as Potts described Nowell. He also gave us a vivid picture of Chattox, who, unlike Demdike, he did actually see in person.

> This Anne Whittle, alias Chattox, was a very old, withered, spent and decrepit creature, her sight almost gone. A dangerous witch of very long continuance, always opposite to Demdike – for whom the one favoured the other hated deadly – and how they envie and accuse one another in their examinations may appear. In her witchcraft always more ready to do mischief to men's goods than themselves, her lips ever chattering and walking – but what she says no man knows.

Chattox claimed that she had been initiated into witchcraft some fourteen years previously by Demdike herself. The Devil had appeared to her in Demdike's house at midnight and asked for her soul. She refused at first, but eventually accepted after 'the great perswassions' of Demdike to do so. The Devil required a place on her body from which to suck blood and he chose, as with Demdike, a spot on her right side near her ribs. She was also visited by a 'spotted Bitch ... which then did speak unto her ... and sayd that she should have Gold, Silver and worldly Wealth, at her will'. At the same time she was given 'Flesh, Butter, Cheese, Bread and Drinke, and bidde eate enough'. After the feast Tibb and Fancie appeared and took away what remained. Interestingly, Chattox noted to Nowell the following: '... although they did eate they were never the fuller, nor better for the same; and that at their said banquet, the said Spirits gave them light to see what they did, although they neyther had fire nor candle light; and that they were both shee Spirites and Devils'.

Despite this event, it is clear that there had been bad blood between the two women and their families for many years. This might explain Chattox's willingness to implicate Demdike to Nowell, when she cited two further deaths in which Demdike had been involved – those of Richard Ashheton of Downham, and Robert Nutter of Greenhead. Chattox also mentioned Demdike's accomplice in these deaths, one 'Widow Lomshawe' who had since died. This would not be the only time this name would come up and it is interesting to speculate here on the vagaries of fate, for had Lomshawe lived she would, no doubt, be as notorious today as Demdike or Chattox.

Nowell now felt that the time had come to act. He had Old Demdike, Old Chattox and her daughter Anne Fedfearne, as well as Alizon Device, committed to the prison in Lancaster Castle.

A Meeting at Malkin Tower

Much of the testimony given in August 1612 hinged on the Witches' Sabbat that was allegedly held on Good Friday, 20 April 1612 at the home of Old Demdike – a dwelling known as Malkin Tower. The origin of this name is a little hard to pin down, but 'malkin' was a term used in the Middle Ages to describe a 'slattern' – a woman of the lowest degree. Quite why it was attached to the grander-sounding 'tower' is a mystery; the dwelling was most probably little more than a cottage and has long since vanished. The supposed purpose of the meeting was to advise and assist an associate of the 'witches' – Jennet Preston, who lived just across the county boundary in Yorkshire – on how best to rid herself, using witchcraft, of local man Thomas Lister who was hounding her due to his belief that she had been responsible for killing his father, another Thomas Lister, five years previously.

Lister senior was a landowner from Gisburn, and he died in dramatic circumstances, having been taken mortally ill very suddenly in 1607, possibly at the wedding of his son. He was heard to cry out, 'Jennet Preston lays heavy upon me!' and similar utterances, before he died. Jennet was then taken to view Thomas' body whereupon the corpse apparently bled at her touch. This was considered at the time to be a sure sign that she had indeed been responsible for his death. Jennet, however, was not tried immediately for the murder but she was clearly in fear for her own life, having been persecuted by Thomas junior. He had attempted to have her convicted of murdering a child by witchcraft, a crime for which she was tried but acquitted. This was the man she supposedly wanted help in bewitching when she appealed for assistance from her friends in Pendle.

For more information on Jennet Preston, as well as the Starkie possessions, there is no better source than Jonathan Lumby's *The Lancashire Witch-Craze*. Lumby's keen eye for detail and his detective ability have helped shape the way the Lancashire cases have come to be viewed and a great debt is owed to him by anyone in search of the historical truth of what was happening in 1612, and of what had gone before.

Jennet Preston's arrest came swiftly after the first damning testimony about the Good Friday Sabbat at Malkin Tower had reached the ears of Roger Nowell in April, and there can be no doubt that he would have wasted little time in relaying news of the horrors he was hearing to his colleagues in Yorkshire. Jennet was arrested and stood trial in York in July before Sir James Altham who, along with Edward Bromley, was one of the principal judges working on the Northern Circuit. She was found guilty and hanged almost one month to the day before the same court arrived in Lancaster.

Much of the evidence given about the Malkin Tower meeting was supplied by two of Elizabeth Device's children: James who was himself a defendant, and Jennet, who was to be the star witness for the prosecution. We do not have accurate information about the ages of either, but Potts put Jennet's age at nine at the time of the trials, and James as older. James was described as an odd job man and a labourer, so must have been old enough to undertake heavy manual labour.

According to James' testimony given to Nowell in spring of 1612, his mother, alarmed at the arrest of her own mother and daughter, organised a meeting, despatching James to steal and kill a sheep which they then cooked and feasted upon at Malkin Tower during the Good Friday gathering. Identified by James as being present at the meeting were several people including Christopher Howgate (Demdike's son) and his wife, along with four other people who were all later arrested and convicted at Lancaster: Katherine Hewitt, John Bulcock and his mother Jane, and Alice Nutter. Their presence was attested not only by James but also by Jennet Device, who was to play a pivotal role in the subsequent trials. Jennet was almost certainly a bastard – the child of a father never named. She was seized upon immediately by Nowell as a potentially invaluable witness. Who better to tell the truth along with all the inside secrets of the family and their nefarious goings-on than an innocent child? Jennet, the youngest in a poverty-stricken and outcast family, must have had a precarious and unpleasant childhood. It was plain to all who later witnessed how her mother screamed at her and threatened her in court, that she was probably mistreated – even if only verbally or by neglect. Given the chance to escape her family, it seems that Jennet Device was a more than willing witness and her testimony proved to be as devastating as Nowell clearly hoped it would be.

Nowell, along with fellow magistrate Nicholas Bannister, interrogated James Device on 27 April. Along with the tale of the Malkin Tower meeting, James talked of hearing 'the voice of a great number of children screiking and crying pittifully' as he approached his grandmother's house one day at twilight. On another occasion he heard the sound of a 'foule yelling like unto a great number of Cattes'. Three nights after this he claimed something came to him while he lay in bed and 'lay upon him very heavily about an hour'. He implicated Alizon in the bewitchment of Henry Bulcock's child, to which she apparently confessed, just as she had after what happened to John Law.

For Nowell, the idea that there were forces at work in his neighbourhood that could defy the laws of nature and create food and light must have been bad enough, but the suggestion of tormented children must have reinforced his belief that the people who stood before him should come to trial. Throughout the history of group persecutions, the link with child abuse is a recurring theme. It was certainly used in accusations against Jews throughout Europe from the time of the First Crusade, and lepers as well as witches were also routinely suspected of such things, as well as of crimes against their communities, such as poisoning the water supply. There is a formula for such persecutions that states, 'fear plus trigger equals scapegoat'. Fear raised its head in Pendle in spring 1612, when something which had been tolerated by the local community for many years was finally exposed as being of a much more sinister nature than anyone had believed possible. The encounter between Alizon Device and John Law had been the trigger, and all that remained was the need to make someone pay.

During this time – her family either fled or imprisoned – it seems that young Jennet Device began to tell her own version of events to Nowell and his colleagues. The question has to be asked why she would do such a thing? Was it the fear of her mother or a way to escape the life she was living, or was it simply because she was a nine-year-old girl, who for the first time was being treated well, given a warm bed to sleep in and enough to eat. In addition, important men were paying attention to her and hanging on every word she uttered. Whatever the reason, her story began to unfold and for those seeking evidence of conspiracy and dark practice there could have been little better. As described here by Thomas Potts, Jennet told Nowell and Bannister about the witches' gathering on that Good Friday:

> ... their Children and Friends being abroad at libertie, laboured a speciall meeting at Malking Tower in the Forrest of Pendle, upon Good Friday, within a weeke after they were committed, of all the most dangerous, wicked, and damnable Witches in the County farre and neere. Upon Good Friday they met, according to solymne appointment, solomnized this great Festivall day according to their former order, with great cheare, merry company, and much conference. In the end, in this great Assemlie, it was decreed M. Covell by reason of his office, shall be slain before the next Assize: The Castle of Lancaster to be blowne up, and ayde and assisitance to be sent to kill M. Lister, with his old enemie and wicked neighbour Jennet Preston ...

So what was actually going on that Good Friday? It is, of course, impossible to say with any degree of certainty, but it is surely probable that some kind of meeting had taken place at Demdike's home. It *may* have been that James stole an animal, which they then feasted upon. But was it a Sabbat? Probably only in the eyes of those who wanted it to be. However, it does make sense that, with the alarming news of the arrests of the two old women, and of Anne Redfearne and Alizon Device, the rest of the family was thrown into a panic. What was more natural than to gather together to try to decide on the best course of action? Jennet Preston and the Bulcocks may well have been friends of the families involved, and Jennet Preston may well have been seeking advice about how best to escape the vengeful pursuit of Thomas Lister junior. Having heard of the arrests and the awful accusations that were being made against them, Alice Nutter might have been visiting out of charity and concern for the family.

In the end of course, they were powerless to do anything – they would hardly have considered attempting to blow up Lancaster Castle in order to free their relatives. It seems that Christopher Howgate took the only sensible decision left to him and his wife and fled the county. Had they stayed they might easily have ended up in the dock as well, facing the rope. But for the remainder this was not an option; they either had no money or nowhere to go to. Perhaps they simply couldn't allow themselves to believe that this was all really happening, and they trusted that it would not touch them personally, even if the authorities *were* tempted to believe all that they were hearing. They might have clung to the hope that the whole horrible mess would blow over and pass them by, leaving them, once the dust had settled, to pick up their lives once more.

And so the meeting might have ended with farewells and hopes for a quick and safe resolution to their troubles. It is not too fanciful to imagine them setting off over the fields in the shadow of Pendle Hill on that Good Friday – Jennet Preston returning to her home and husband in Gisburn, John and Jane Bulcock picking their way through the twilight, Alice Nutter – her thoughts focused on the plight of the poor and friendless people she was leaving – returning to the relative luxury of her home at Roughlee, while Katherine Hewitt started off on the journey back to her husband John in Colne. They could not have realised the full horror of their situation, or suspected that these were to be their very last days of freedom; that soon the awful might of the law would swing into action and carry them away to a fate they could never have expected, and did not deserve.

Part Three: The Assize

Lancaster was the centre for the administration of law and the punishment of crime for the entire county, a position it was to hold until well into the nineteenth century; the county was then known as Lancaster, Lancashire being a much more recent name. The assizes were held in the castle twice a year, in spring and autumn, and these courts dealt with cases passed up from the Quarter Sessions and those of sufficient seriousness to merit a hearing before the judges for the Northern Circuit. The great medieval stronghold dominated the town below, with the gatehouse acting as the main entrance through which all prisoners, including those of 1612, would have passed. The court where trials took place at this time was demolished in about 1800, to be replaced by a court which still functions today as a crown court, hearing criminal cases on a daily basis. This court occupies the same space within the castle as did its predecessor, and although the old Norman Dungeon Tower was swept away during the refurbishments of the nineteenth century, the holding cells below the court still exist, as does the Well or Witches' Tower, that was to be home to the defendants for the next months as they awaited their trials and the arrival of the judges.

The Judges: Altham and Bromley

Sir Edward Bromley was a Shropshire gentleman and the nephew of an ex-Lord Chancellor – the man who, incidentally, had overseen the trial and execution of Mary, Queen of Scots. He was a Baron of the Exchequer and had actually presided at the Lent Assize in York in 1611, where Jennet Preston had appeared on a charge of murdering a child by witchcraft for which she had been acquitted. Jennet Preston was actually to play a key role in the Pendle case, even though she was dead before it began. Jennet's second trial, in York in July for the murder of Thomas Lister senior, brought her before Bromley's colleague on the Northern Circuit, Sir James Altham, who sentenced her to death, and her uneasy spirit seemed to haunt the proceedings in Lancaster throughout the trials. It seems that, by the time the two men reached Lancaster, the trial of Jennet Preston and the verdict handed down by Altham was already being called into question. Certainly her family was loud in its condemnation. This has led some people to wonder if the publication of the trials in Lancaster and their referencing of *Daemonolgie* perhaps stemmed from a desire to justify the convictions in the face of the accusations levelled against Altham in York. This may actually be the reason why Altham did not preside over the trials in Lancaster, instead leaving the task entirely to his more junior colleague Sir Edward Bromley.

Of the two men, Altham appears to have been the hard-liner when it came to cases involving witchcraft, Recusancy or religious heresy. Altham had come to the attention of the king for his defence of the established church and his treatment of those who deviated from its teachings. In 1611 he had been chosen to sit on the trial of two men accused of heresy in London, both of whom he condemned and saw burnt at the stake. If anything, of the two men, Bromley was considered the more lenient judge. After the assize in Lancaster, of course, this was to change radically. However, it seems that Bromley went through a great deal of heart-searching before presiding in Lancaster, and we should not ignore the possibility that these men truly believed in the existence of manifest evil within their society, which they saw as their duty to eradicate.

Thomas Potts

This is not to say that there were no ulterior motives at work, or that what Potts wrote was a true record of what went on at the assize, either with regard to the events in Pendle itself or at Read Hall in the spring of 1612. When we read through Potts' tract, we become aware of an undoubted tendency to embellish and editorialise for the benefit of his readership, as well as a strong bias against the defendants, in favour of the authorities. Roger Nowell and the two judges are painted in terms that are almost hagiographic, but far from being any kind of justification or excuse for the verdicts or the nature and conduct of the prosecution of the cases, this simply represents a well-documented tradition in such reports and transcripts, one which continued for at least another two centuries.

Such an elite view so strongly argued also had the effect of reinforcing the views of the lower strata of society: if learned men, and indeed the king himself, believed in the existence of witches, then who were they to disagree? And so alongside the grass-roots fear and superstition of the people who had lived alongside the Pendle accused, there was also surely a political element to the proceedings. These trials, and others like them, were a perfect public forum in which the authorities could emphasise the messages they wanted to get across. Ultimately, of course, all we have left to us of this extraordinary trial and the events that led up to it, are the words of Mr Potts. His is a suspect and no doubt flawed account, but it is still one which, read with this in mind, may still yield up a picture of the way the world worked in seventeenth-century England. Potts was constrained to some extent, however, to keep his embellishments within reasonable limits: the official court records (now long since vanished) were in the public domain, and there were also plenty of people who had witnessed the trials for themselves, and who knew what had, and had not, been said. But in the end it is Potts' account to which we must look. It is his world we must enter in order to catch a glimpse of the extraordinary events that took place in Lancaster Castle four hundred years ago.

The Accused

On the afternoon of Sunday 16 August 1612, Judge Bromley and Judge Altham arrived, tired and dusty, from the Westmorland Assizes. It is fair to say that some of the most intriguing and notorious trials in English history were about to begin.

Altogether, there were nine defendants from the Pendle area, a further eight from Salmesbury, Margaret Pearson from Padiham and Isobel Roby, who came from Windle:

From Pendle –	Anne Whittle (Old Chattox)
	Elizabeth Device (Old Demdike's daughter)
	James and Alizon Device (Elizabeth's children)
	Anne Redfearne (Old Chattox's daughter)

	Alice Nutter
	Katherine Hewitt
	John and Jane Bulcock (mother and son)
From Padiham –	Margaret Pearson
From Samlesbury –	Jennet Bierley
	Elen Bierley
	Jane Southworth
	John Ramsden
	Elizabeth Astley
	Isobel Sidegraves
	Lawrence Haye
From Windle –	Isobel Roby

N.B. Alice Grey was listed as one of the Samlesbury defendants but she was actually accused, along with Katherine Hewitt, of murdering Ann Foulds, for which crime she was found *not* guilty. Potts gave no account of her trial and she only appeared once more in the pamphlet, on a list of people acquitted.

It must be said that we really know very little about these people except what has come to us from the viewpoint of those whose task it was to prosecute them. The poor throughout history have lived their lives hidden from posterity. They left no wills or diaries, had no voice in which to speak to us from years past. We can only guess, based on what we know of the times and the experiences of others whose lives were better documented, what kind of existence they might have led. It seems clear that many of the families involved in the Pendle case were living on the breadline, in complete poverty, and with little or no education and few prospects. It may well be that the apparent willingness to confess on the part of the accused reflects the fact that all they had to ensure that they did not starve was the fear they were able to inspire in their better-off neighbours. We have seen this at work with, for example, John Device, Elizabeth's own husband, who was terrified of Chattox, and who died believing himself to have been her victim. Why did he not go to Demdike for help? Why did his own wife – if she were the monster Potts clearly believed her to be – not intervene to save him? Today, we would say that the reason for this was that none of these people were actually what they professed to be, of course, and that witchcraft does not exist.

But the mind is a powerful tool, and there are some things so deeply rooted in the human psyche that the rational mind cannot contend with them. It is possible to frighten oneself to death. If this is so, then it is as easy to believe that the withered old harridan who had been refused money, or milk, or bread, could, in retribution, cause physical harm. It may be that the accused actually believed that they did indeed possess some kind of supernatural power. When it came to trying to get the authorities off their backs they may even have believed that the simplest course of action was to admit to whatever they were accused of. It may also be part of the reason why so much additional information seems to have been given so freely, information that was to drag men and women who were nothing to do with the two families at the heart of the case, into the whole sorry mess. Whatever the underlying reasons and circumstances that had brought them to Lancaster Castle, their day in court had finally arrived.

The Trials: 18–19 August 1612

Trials in this period differed greatly from the modern examples we are familiar with. The most notable difference was a lack of defence counsel. The judge himself was expected to be impartial, and, in effect, ensure a fair trial for the defendant who would then be judged by a jury of twelve men typically chosen from the middle ranks of local society. Potts described how the jury was selected:

> My lord Bromley commanded M Sherrifs of the Countie of Lancaster in open court to returne a Jurie of worthy sufficient Gentlemen of understanding, to pass between our Sovereign Lord the Kinges Majestie, and her, and others the Prisoners, upon their lives and deaths; as hereafter follow in court; who were sfterwards sworne, according to the forme and order of the Court, the Prisoners being admitted to their lawful charges

Theirs was a difficult and unenviable task. Over the coming two days they would sit in judgement on the defendants and hear tales that must have been far removed from their everyday lives. But while their job was to hand down the verdicts, there was no doubt that they would have looked to the presiding judge for guidance, and it does seem that Bromley had taken advice on what to look for in order to convict a witch; meaning, in effect, that the Pendle defendants were left to face their ordeal alone. It is hard to imagine what they must have felt, emerging from the darkness of their prison, filthy, dishevelled and confused, only to be brought before the majesty of the law and the eyes of their neighbours.

The assize began on Monday 17 August, under the eye of Sir Edward Bromley, and the first of the many trials for witchcraft was that of Anne Whittle – Old Chattox herself – which took place on the second day of the sitting. Chattox was, we have been told, old and decrepit, and must have looked every inch the part of the wicked old witch as she was brought into court. Potts realised that her pitiful state might have tempted some to sympathy and begins his account of her trial with a disclaimer:

> The example of this poore creature would have moved pitie, in respect of her great contrition and repentence, after she was committed to the Castle at Lancaster until the coming of the judges of assize. But such was the multitude of her crying sinnes, as it took away all sense of humanity. And the repetition of her hellish practices, and revenge, being the chiefest things in which she alwayes took great delight, together with a particular declaration of the Murders shee had committed, layde open to the world; and given in Evidence against her at the time of her Arraignment and Tryall; as certainly did it beget contempt in the Audience, and such as she never offended.

There have been various attempts to ascribe the origin of Anne Whittle's nickname, but the simplest explanation is surely that, as happens in great old age, she was in the habit of talking to herself. Bent and withered as she was, this must have alarmed anyone who already harboured suspicions about her intent.

Potts gave us the text of a charm Old Chattox was supposed to have used to take the curse off some drink at the home of John Moore:

> Three Biters hast thou bitten
> The Hart, ill Eye, ill Tonge:
> Three bitter shall be thy Boote,
> Father, Sonne and Holy Ghost

> A God's name.
> Five Pater-nosters, five Avies'
> and a Creede
> in worship of five wounds
> of our Lord.

There is reference here to the Five Wounds, which itself had been the basis of a popular pious cult in the Middle Ages. Moore's wife had chided the old woman, presumably for the use of such language, and Chattox had taken offence, cursing their milk cow so that it went mad and died six weeks later. It is easy to see how the use of archaic, suspect terms, 'Avies, Pater-Nosters and Creedes', with their obvious Catholic associations, might well have sown unease in anyone who heard them.

The Trial of Anne Whittle

Anne Whittle was indicted as follows:

> This Anne Whittle, alias Chattox, of the Forrest of Pendle in the Countie of Lancaster Widdow, being Indicted, for that shee feloniously had practised, used, and exercised divers wicked and divelish Artes called Witchcraftes, Inchauntments, Charmes, and Sorceries, in and upon one Robert Nutter of Greenhead, in the county of Lancaster: and by force of the same Witchcraft, feloniously the sayd Robert Nutter had killed, Contra Pacem.

Chattox pleaded not guilty and, as was the custom, 'put herself upon God and her Country' (i.e. the jury) in the hope of a just deliverance. The trial began with a reading of the testimony given at Read before Roger Nowell, which, of course, contained not only the damning evidence against her given by Demdike and others, but also her own confession. Much of the evidence concentrated on the death of Robert Nutter and the key testimony regarding the events leading up to Nutter's demise was given by James Robinson, who had lived for a time with Nutter's grandfather. The events dated back some eighteen years, but Robinson remembered how, while visiting his grandfather in the summer, Robert Nutter had fallen ill. Nutter said at the time that he believed himself to be the victim of Chattox's malice. He had also accused Chattox's daughter, Anne Redfearne, of bewitching him. Both, said Robinson, were 'commonly reputed and reported to bee Witches', and he cited instances of milk turning sour at their touch. Robert recovered and left soon after for Wales, saying to his grandfather that, 'If ever he came againe he would get his father to put the said Redfearne out of his house, or he himselfe would pull it downe'. Trying to calm the young man down, Thomas Redfearne told him that he would no doubt 'be in a better minde' when he returned. But Nutter was never to return. According to Robinson, Robert Nutter died in Cheshire en route for Pendle, just before Candlemas (The Feast of the Purification of the Virgin on 2 February) the following year.

The evidence, not of all of which Potts saw fit to include in his tract, was flimsy enough on the face of it. He often referred to this 'missing' evidence as though it was already in the common domain, and it may well have been, perhaps in the form of an official document. However, this has long been lost along with every other official record of the proceedings, and so these references have become all the more tantalising for the modern reader. Without a doubt their absence (frustrating in the extreme for the modern historian) shrouds the trials in an ever-thickening layer of mystery.

Perhaps in an attempt at mitigation, Chattox testified that Robert had tried to seduce Anne – 'To have his pleasure of her' as she put it – and that when Anne refused he went away 'in a great rage'.

It seems clear that Nutter threatened Anne and her mother with eviction when the time eventually came for him to inherit the land they rented from the Nutter family. Chattox told the court that she had summoned Fancie and told him to avenge her. It seems that Robert had other enemies, because Chattox went on to say that she, along with one Jane Boothman and the ubiquitous Widow Lomshawe, had been approached by Elizabeth Nutter, Robert's grandmother, to take his life so that she could inherit the land in his stead. Apparently the three agreed to this request, but Chattox was dissuaded from carrying it out at that time by the intercession of Anne's husband Thomas Redfearne. Lomshawe had been so furious that she wanted Redfearne dead, but she too calmed down, apparently after a talk from the local school-master, Baldwin. Thomas was so grateful that he gave the man a capon. It was, however, but a reprieve for Robert, and within three months he was dead.

Chattox told the court that she believed that Boothman and Lomshawe had been just as culpable of his death. Both the women had since died and of course this outburst did nothing to help Chattox's case, and neither did evidence read out from James Device's testimony. In the extract given in evidence against her, the court heard how she had robbed graves in Newchurch of scalps and teeth – later found at her home – and how clay images had been discovered, made by her to bring about the death of Anne Nutter. Alizon Device corroborated this, describing how Chattox believed Anne had been laughing at her one day, as she stood talking to Alizon. Furious, Chattox had cursed her, and within three weeks Anne was dead. Faced with this evidence Chattox broke down, and 'with weeping teares she humbly acknowledged [the evidence] to be true and cried out unto God for Mercy and forgivenesse of her sinnes, and humbly prayed my Lord to be mercifull unto Anne Redfearne her daughter'.

The Trial of Elizabeth Device

Chattox was removed and Elizabeth Device, Demdike's daughter, replaced her in the dock. Elizabeth was charged on three counts of murder, those of brothers John and James Robinson and, along with Alice Nutter, that of Henry Mitton. Elizabeth was known as 'Squinting Lizzie' because one eye was set higher than the other – 'a preposterous marke of nature' as Potts described it. Her trial was to provide excitement enough for everyone present, and provoke rage in Thomas Potts. Her greatest sin in his eyes seems to have been, in the first instance, a refusal to confess. Having finally made some kind of statement to Roger Nowell and Nicholas Banister in April, she then had the temerity to deny it. She was clearly over-wrought at her trial, especially when confronted by her own daughter, Jennet, who was brought in to testify against her. Potts was vitriolic in his utter condemnation of this woman:

> O barbarous and inhumane Monster, beyond example; so farre from sensible understanding of thy owne miserie, as to bring thy owne naturall children into mischiefe and bondage; and thy selfe to be a witness upon the Gallowes, to see thy owne children, by they devilish instructions hatcht up in Villanie and Witchcraft, to suffer with thee, even in the beginning of their time, a shamefull and untimely Death. ... it is very certaine, that amongst all these witches there was not a more dangerous and devillish Witch to execute mischiefe, having old Demdike, her mother, to assist her : James Device and Alizon Device, her owne natural children, all provided with Spirits, upon any occasion of offence readie to assist her.

A great deal of Potts' outrage seemed to stem from the meeting Elizabeth allegedly masterminded at Malkin Tower on Good Friday 1612, where it was decided, so he insisted, to blow up the castle and kill its govenor Thomas Covell. Again he was affronted by the fact that Elizabeth should dare deny this happened, even after she had, seemingly, admitted that the meeting itself had taken place. But, luckily for Potts 'it pleased God to raise up a yong maid, Jennet Device, her own daughter, about the age of nine yeares (a witnesse unexpected) to discover all their Practises, Meetings, Consultations, Murthers, Charmes and Villanies'. And testify Jennet did, with devastating results. From the moment Jennet was brought into court Elizabeth began, in what we are told was her usual manner, to scream at the girl 'in such fearefull manner, as all the court did not a little wonder at her, and so amazed the child, as with weeping teares shee cryed out unto my Lord the Judge, and told him shee was not able to speak in the presence of her mother'.

Nothing could calm Elizabeth and finally the judge ordered her removed from the dock. Jennet was placed on a table in full view of the court, and there, the absolute centre of attention, she began to tell how her mother was a witch whose familiar spirit was a brown dog named Ball.

Jennet professed that on three occasions she had heard her mother ask Ball to kill, first John, then James Robinson, and finally Henry Mitton, each death occurring within the space of three weeks of the initial command. Evidence given by James Device to Nowell in April corroborated this testimony. Apparently, Mitton had died for refusing Demdike a penny. She had brought about the death of John Robinson by making a clay model of him and then slowly crumbling it over the course of several days. As the image crumbled, so Robinson's life ebbed away until he died. As important (if not more so for Potts) was the meeting at Malkin Tower on Good Friday 1612, which had been organised by Elizabeth. The testimony taken by Nowell was read out and was corroborated by that given by both James and Jennet. Each of them named people who were supposedly present at the meeting, including John and Jane Bulcock, Katherine Hewitt ('Mouldheels') and Alice Nutter, as well as the children's uncle Christopher Howgate and his wife.

James told how Jennet Preston had promised them all a great celebration at her home in a year's time, once her purpose with Thomas Lister was achieved. She and several others had left the meeting mounted on ponies of differing hues before vanishing into thin air before his eyes, horses and all. Elizabeth was obviously now in the dock once more, because having heard the evidence against her she cried out for mercy and was taken away, her trial over. Her fate was plainly sealed on little more than hearsay and gossip, and the imaginings of her own offspring, one of whom – her son James – was brought into court himself to face the same kind of swift justice.

The Trial of James Device

James was charged with causing the death by witchcraft of Anne Towneley and John Duckworth. 'A wicked and miserable wretch' was Pott's description of James Device, who was obviously ailing when he was tried; we are told that he was unable to walk unaided, stand or even speak. Potts was unable to account for his condition, which had led some observers to the conclusion that James had been tortured.

There is some basis to this supposition, for, unusually, we have a record of the questioning James underwent at the hands of Thomas Covell and others while he was a prisoner in Lancaster Castle. The answers James gave them, however, differed little from those he had given to Roger Nowell on 27 April. Covell mentioned the 'great paines' he himself had taken 'to discover his practices, and other such witches as he knew to bee dangerous'. Whatever happened to James, whether illness or mistreatment, it is difficult to see how a person – who was presumably in his late teens or perhaps early twenties and who earned his money labouring – could be

reduced to the wreck described by Potts. The best Potts could come up with was that James had starved himself or otherwise done himself harm, in an attempt to commit suicide in a bid to escape 'just judgement'. It was entirely possible that his months in prison had left him ill or deranged; it was also possible that James, being the only male defendant from the Demdike brood, was singled out for more rough treatment while in the hands of his captors.

We will never know the truth, but what we do know is that his physical condition notwithstanding, James was placed on trial for the murders of Anne Towneley and John Duckworth, and also for causing the death by witchcraft of John and Blaze Hargreaves of Goldsheybooth. Tantalisingly, Potts told us that, rather than go through all the testimony given against James, he would confine himself to that which appeared in the 'Records of the Crown' with regard to the case; records which, of course, have long since vanished from the public domain. Potts contented himself with the comment that James 'never tooke felicitie in any things, but in revenge, blood and mischiefe'.

Interestingly, Potts was at pains in James' case to emphasise the legality of the proceedings. Although there appeared to be enough evidence in his testimony for Nowell to convict him, Judge Bromley stated that the prisoner had the right to hear the evidence in person, and called the witnesses to court to speak in James' presence.

We hear, in James' own words, that on one particular 'Sheare' Thursday (Maundy Thursday) he had been instructed by Demdike to take Communion, but not to eat the bread. Instead he would be approached on the way home from church and was to give the Host (sacramental bread) to whatever manner of thing asked him for it. This piece of evidence would have had immediate connotations with stories told of supposed Host Desecration by the Jews of Medieval Europe, thus linking the accused to a long tradition of perceived anti-Christian activity. In the end the creature that approached James Device as he returned from church was a hare, and it was so furious to discover that James had eaten the bread that it threatened to pull him to pieces. James was approached four days later at Newchurch by a dog, which asked James for his soul. Despite James telling the dog that his soul was not his to give, he still offered the creature 'as much as was in him to give'.

Two days later James had an altercation with Mistress Towneley at her home. She accused him and his mother of stealing and hit James in the back. Some time later a black dog appeared to him and reminded him of Mistress Towneley's behaviour towards him. It told James to fashion a model of the woman in clay, bake it and then crumble it. Within two days of the clay picture having being destroyed, Anne Towneley was dead. Giving evidence against her half-brother at his trial, Jennet told the court that James had named his dog Dandy, and that the familiar had helped bring about the deaths of both the Hargreaves men, although what they had supposedly done to upset James was not revealed.

James was clearly seen locally as someone to avoid crossing: John Duckworth supposedly lost his life because he refused to give James an old shirt he had promised him. It may be that James had seen how well his family's methods of intimidating their neighbours into supporting them had worked, and had used his own physical youth and strength to coerce people into giving him what he wanted. James Device may well have been unpopular, even disliked, but in the end all the evidence against him was constructed on hearsay – a confession that may well have been illegally obtained and tall tales built on fear and suspicion.

Nowell's evidence was then submitted, and most of it concerned the meeting at Malkin Tower on Good Friday. James had admitted to stealing a lamb for the feast. Again, we hear of the plot to help Jennet Preston kill Thomas Lister in Yorkshire, the presence of the Howgates, and of the Bulcocks. A prayer was recited in court by

Jennet, which she ascribed to her brother. It was a charm to remove a bewitchment, and the effect it must have had on a no doubt hushed audience must have been sensational.

The evidence complete, the jury retired to consider its verdict on the day's three defendants. We have no indication of the length of time the deliberations took, but we are told that when the jury returned it was to convict Anne Whittle, Elizabeth Device and her son James, on all counts.

The Witches of Samlesbury

Thomas Potts then turned his attention to the trial of three women from Samlesbury, which took place on 19 August. Chronologically, this trial actually followed the first trial of Anne Refearne (for the murder of Robert Nutter) which took place on the afternoon of Tuesday 18 August. Potts recorded no details about this trial when he returned to the Pendle case later, except to report that Anne had been acquitted for lack of evidence. Instead, he dedicated the next, quite considerable, portion of his narrative to the extraordinary saga of the 'Samlesbury Witches'.

The parallels between the two cases are many and obvious, and, while some of the evidence given in this trial is similar to that in the Pendle case, there is clearly much more to this tale of a murdered baby and an abused teenager than at first meets the eye. Once more, the primary witness in the case was a young girl, this time fourteen-year-old Grace Sowerbutts. Again there was talk of murder, and of mysterious midnight meetings with beings plainly not of this earth. But right from the start there was a different tenor to the tale. Much of the story as told by Grace was a jumble of comings and goings, with little real evidence of witchcraft, at least not as those present would have understood it. The reason for this was later revealed in court, but that too has to be re-examined in light of what we know of the times, and with an understanding of the motives of those who staged what was, in fact, something of a show trial. In the end it was to be the Catholic Church and the Recusant community that was on trial, not merely three hapless victims of politics and propaganda.

We must also examine the attitude Potts took to the case. While he described Jennet Device as a God-given gift, sent to help in the eradication of evil, he saw Grace Sowerbutts (once the 'truth' is made evident, of course) as a mere catspaw in a Catholic conspiracy. To begin with, Potts gave the evidence – as Grace gave it – in much the same tone of outrage and appalled disbelief he used when describing the Pendle trials. He was disparaging of the three women who stood accused of 'Witchcraft upon the body of Grace Sowerbutts': Jane Southworth, a relative by marriage of the Southworths of Samlesbury Hall, Jennet Bierley, Grace's grandmother, and Ellen Bierley, her aunt, and one has to wonder why he did this, given the final outcome – a point we shall return to later.

Of the remaining accused Potts listed earlier in the book, it seems that they were found not guilty at some stage prior to the trial which took place on 19 August. Having said that the accused who had been acquitted in this case were certainly not treated as though innocent. Given that they had been in prison throughout the summer along with the others, they received no apology. Instead, the judge gave them a talking to, more or less indicating that they had been lucky to escape. In the end he bound them over 'notwithstanding the judgement of the court' on payment of 'sufficient Sueries, to appear at the next assize at Lancaster, and in the meantime to be of good behaviour'.

The testimony of Grace Sowerbutts as recounted by Potts was a confused account of numerous abductions of the girl by the three women accused, plus another she named as 'Old Doewife'. It seems that Grace was regularly whisked away into barns and haylofts, and her accounts even hinted at sexual abuse, of being laid on by some unknown force before she was then found, whereupon she spent the next few days in bed in a state of insensibility. She told of her grandmother transforming into a dog before her eyes, and of how, while in this form, she urged Grace to drown herself.

Grace's most damning accusation, however, was that Jane and Ellen Bierley had brought about the death of a twelve-month-old baby – the child of Thomas Walshman. According to Grace's testimony, they took the child from its parents' bed and drove a nail into its navel to enable them to suck its blood, whereupon the child 'did thenceforth languish, and not long after dyed'. Not content with this, they then dug up the body and took it to Jane's home, where they cooked and ate its flesh before rendering what remained so that they could anoint themselves in order to be able to change shape. Invited to partake of the feast, Grace refused.

She also spoke of meetings at Red Bank with 'four black things, going upright, and yet not like men in the face' with whom the women ate and danced, before the spirits 'did pull downe the said three women and did abuse their bodies' – this time including Grace in their carnal entertainments. Chillingly, Grace told of a great gathering of women who she believed 'lived on the North-side of Ribble'. Clearly these women, according to Grace, were all involved in witchcraft and it is not difficult to believe that she would have named names had things not suddenly turned against her.

Reading the account as told by Potts one cannot but ponder on the nature of the evidence. It is very much darker, infinitely nastier and somehow alien to that which routinely appears in English trials. Reading other accounts of witch trials, particularly those that took place in East Anglia where accusations were rife, the kind of evidence that was given against the Samlesbury accused is rare indeed. It is somehow not native. It is too horrible – if that isn't a contradiction in terms. Even according to Potts there was nothing from neighbours or relatives, no accusations going back in time, no unexplained deaths or instances of threats or deviant behaviour. The best the prosecution could offer seemed to be that old Sir John Southworth, since deceased, believed that Jane was a witch, and that he always avoided her whenever he could. There were actually grave doubts that the man ever even knew Jane; indeed he may well have died prior to her wedding with his kinsman. That hardly mattered, of course, once Potts revealed the 'truth' behind this case, as it doubtless pleased the authorities to present it.

The entire charade was now dramatically revealed as the work of a Catholic priest (worse still, a Jesuit) known as Thompson – in fact none other than Christopher Southworth, a relative of Jane's by her marriage. The Southworths have a long and fascinating history, especially during this period, when one half of the family became Anglican while the other remained Catholic.

Later in the century there was to be a saint among the Catholic half of the family – John – who is buried in Westminster Cathedral. John was executed after being arrested by his own Southworth cousin. Of the Christopher Southworth implicated in the trials of 1612, however, little is known, but the authorities claimed at the trial that he had coached the child in what to say, with the intent that three innocent and God-fearing (Protestant) women would be executed. His motive? They had attended an Anglican Church despite his attempt to convert them back to Rome. Potts' denouement was a magnificent example of sycophancy and hyperbole. He managed to implicate the Catholic Church, expose a devilish plot, set an example to the recalcitrant people of Lancashire, and praise the judge, all in one sweeping statement.

The women, given the chance to speak by the judge, fell on their knees and begged that Grace be questioned about who had 'set her on' to make the accusations against them. The girl could only answer that 'shee was put to a Master to learn'.

Immediately the judge told the court that 'if a Priest or Jesuit had a hand in one end of it, there would appeare to bee knaverie, and practises in the other end of it'. He ordered the girl to be removed from her father – who was naturally a suspect in the plot – and had her committed to the care of William Leigh and Edward Chisnal, JPs for the county, who were charged with the task of rooting out the truth.

According to the report made to the court by Chisnal and Leigh, Grace recanted all her previous allegations, putting the blame on the man who had coached her in what to say – Christopher Southworth. The court readily accepted this testimony and, once the 'truth' was revealed, Potts stated that it was obvious all along because the priest had not done his job very well at all. He had mixed up the face with the foot when it came to describing the black-shaped spirits Grace had encountered, because everyone knew that these beings looked like men (he even quoted Old Chattox as an authority on this – Fancie being fair of face) and that they actually had cloven hooves. Everyone also 'knew', of course, that witches had familiar spirits in the shape of dogs – they did not become dogs themselves. Potts mockingly stated that the plot failed due to these inaccuracies, and claimed that it was hastily hatched on the back of the first arrests in Pendle, back in April. Also, the fact that the accused – having done their evil as far as they could on her – then invited Grace to join in their rites was totally inconsistent with the practice of witchcraft. This was especially the case with regard to the supposed murder of the child – a murder Potts believed was so horrible that even 'The Witches of the Forrest of Pendle were never so cruell nor so barbarous' as to commit. Potts was in transports of delight over the discovery of the plot and its outcome, particularly as it allowed him even more scope to praise Bromley:

> Thus were these poore Innocent creatures, by the great care and paines of this honourable Judge, delivered from the danger of this conspiracie; this bloudie practis of the priest laid open. These are but ordinary with Priests and Jesuits: no respect of Bloud, kindred, or friendship, can move them to forbeare their Conspiracies: for when he had laboured treacherously to seduce and convert them, and yet could doe no good; then devised he this meanes.

Seemingly unconcerned that the group from Pendle was slowly but surely being convicted on very similar evidence (without the hint of Catholic Conspiracy to save them) he begged that:

> God if his great mercie deliver us all from them and their damnable conspiracies: and when any of his Majesties subjects, so free and innocent as these, shall come in question, grant them as honourable a Triall, as Reverend and worthy a Judge to sit upon them; and in the end as speedie a deliverance.

A warning had been given to all and sundry to be on their guard against such plots, and, content that the wicked purpose of a Jesuit had been thwarted, the jury retired. It swiftly returned with the inevitable 'not guilty' verdict.

There are many points of interest here. Firstly, why would a priest go to such lengths to invent evidence against these women? True, there was a vague family connection, but Jane Southworth was not a prominent member of the family, and there seems to be no obvious connection between Christopher Southworth and either of the Bierley women.

Secondly, why go to such lengths to gain supposed revenge for his failure to convert them? Had this been the case there were surely better targets and plenty of them – half the population of Lancashire, in fact.

Thirdly, why coach a child in such transparent lies? As a Jesuit, Southworth would have been well educated in the finer points of continental-style witchcraft, and yet he told her nothing of Sabbats of night-flying, of familiars, of the Devil's mark. Some commentators have interpreted the Red Bank meeting as a Sabbat, but it reads, in fact, more like the working of a fevered adolescent imagination, and the description bears no hint of the actual practice of witchcraft.

And fourthly, why would this man risk arrest and execution over so trivial a matter? Had he been apprehended, Southworth faced death by hanging, drawing and quartering: for him to have exposed himself to this danger there had to be motive beyond mere pique – surely. The whole thing reeks of a plot, yes, but it would make more sense if it was actually a plot concocted by the very people who arrested and imprisoned the Samlesbury suspects, based on the hysterical fantasies of a disturbed and suggestible adolescent girl.

The arrests of the Samlesbury suspects followed hard upon the heels of the arrests in Pendle. This was a good time to make an accusation, and it may be that the delusional Grace, and probably her father as well, were riding on the tails of what was clearly going to become a *cause celebre*. We know that Jennet Bierley was Grace's grandmother, which would make Thomas Sowerbutts her son-in-law, and we cannot rule out personal vendetta as a motive. Was the original accusation then hijacked by the authorities without the Sowerbutts even realising it? Here was a chance to discredit the Catholic Church, and perhaps the naming of a Southworth priest was no accident either.

There is certainly a suggestion that this entire 'Popish Plot' (not the only one given credence in the paranoid seventeenth century, by any means) was constructed by the authorities at a very early stage. If so, then the Samlesbury witch trial was a show-trial, its outcome already determined, and this indicates that the authorities wanted to use this public arena to highlight the threat of the Catholic Church in Lancashire. The county was the heartland of the faith. If The Establishment could tar the many priests risking their lives in Lancashire with the same brush and make people afraid of them, then might they not, perhaps, wean any potential converts away from their influence and even persuade them to turn over any priests already in their midst? This would explain the artless way Potts reported the case. Always assuming that he knew about this, of course (and that he was not just another convenient prop in the drama), Potts would have had to go along with the concept that this was a genuine accusation, in order for the surprise revealed at its end to appear valid.

And if this is true then the accused were victims twice over. The women who actually stood trial along with the others already acquitted (but not, remember, completely exonerated) had spent the summer in the dungeon of the Well Tower, had been dragged from their homes and families and hauled through the courts in terror of their lives. Were they actually political rather than religious pawns? Even if we discount this as a theory and there ever was some 'knavish' priest bent upon their destruction as convicted witches, they certainly suffered enough because of it. But all we know of the events comes to us, once again, via Thomas Potts, and there is no corroboration for any of it – not with the Pendle suspects, and certainly not with what went on in Samlesbury. As with so much else we will probably never know the truth, and there is no clear evidence one way or the other.

Having concluded the sensational trial of the Samlesbury accused, and without a hint that he was even aware of his double-standards and outright hypocrisy, Potts now turned the spotlight back to the Pendle case.

The Trial Of Anne Redfearne

Potts' account of the trial of Anne Redfearne is one of the shortest in the book. The evidence against her seemed to have been virtually non-existent, as witnessed by her acquittal on the first charge in a trial that took place on the afternoon of the previous day. She stood trial again on Wednesday 19 August – just after the acquittal of the three Samlesbury suspects – and one might have expected that she too would be found not guilty, given the dearth of evidence on the second count.

Accused of bringing about the death of Christopher Nutter (the man she had been cleared of murdering, and a crime for which her mother had already been convicted) some eighteen years previously, Anne pleaded not guilty. Potts described Anne as 'more dangerous than her Mother', and of being responsible for 'many strange practices'. In fact, he produced nothing to back up this claim, and it seems that Anne was sent to her death on little more evidence than hazy memories in the minds of the family and friends of the deceased.

John Nutter told of returning home to Pendle with his brother Robert and father Christopher some eighteen years past, at which time his brother had spoken of his fears. Robert believed that Chattox and Anne had bewitched him, and was in mortal fear of them both. Christopher chided him, calling him a 'foolish Ladde', but Robert was so afraid that he was ready to go to Sir Richard Shuttleworth with his accusations. He wanted the two women to be taken to Lancaster Castle and 'laid where they shall be glad to bite lice in two with their teeth'. Within a short space of time, as we have already heard, Robert was dead. At no time do we hear why Anne might have had reason to wish Robert's father Christopher Nutter to become ill. Indeed, his seems to have been the voice of reason to some extent, and the only evidence concerning his

death was that supplied by Margaret Crook, Christopher's daughter, in a statement to Roger Nowell. It seems that after Robert's demise Christopher too became ill. He languished for a time, before dying at Martinmas (11 November) of the year after. According to Margaret, Christopher 'did sundry times say, that hee was bewitched', but he refused to ever name anyone.

With such scant evidence concerning this supposed murder, it seems that Anne was convicted, in the main, of fashioning clay images, a task at which she was supposedly acknowledged to be a master, by no less a person than Old Demdike herself. Demdike, of course, was the sworn enemy of Chattox; she would surely have had no compunction about implicating a member of her old adversary's family.

James Device's testimony was also referred to, and he too implicated Anne, telling how he had seen her fashioning clay 'pictures', half a yard long at her home, and of being confronted nearby by 'a thing like a Hare, which spit fire at him'. Yet again Potts reserved his ire for another woman who refused to confess, and who went to her death without once repenting, or admitting her crimes. His typically sanctimonious account of her trial ended with these words: 'no meanes could move her to repentance, for as shee lived, so shee dyed'.

The Trial of Alice Nutter

Alice Nutter, in her own way, has become as famous as Demdike or Chattox, albeit for entirely different reasons. The first of the defendants who was not part of the Demdike or Chattox broods, Alice was set apart from the bulk of the other defendants. Described by Potts as a 'rich woman [of] great estate and [with] children of good hope', she was not as easy to overlook or hurry through the courts as the rest might have been.

Potts' remark about her social station has influenced several writers to assume that there were ulterior motives behind her accusation. These range from greed on the part of her son, Miles, who was keen to inherit her wealth, to a quarrel over property with Roger Nowell, to a modern concept that has Alice a martyr for the Catholic faith. The two former theories, neither of which have any solid evidence to back them up, have been given unwarranted credence by Robert Neill in his fanciful novel *Mist Over Pendle*, and before him by the great Victorian Romanticist Harrison Ainsworth in *The Lancashire Witches*. While artistic licence is perfectly valid in fiction, of course, it is a shame that so many people have read these accounts and accepted them as the truth.

Turning to Potts we find a brief account of Alice's social station and an attempt to understand why a woman in her position would allow herself to become entangled with witchcraft in the first place. Potts made a rare reference to *Daemonologie* here. Although he did not state this openly, it would have been obvious to anyone familiar with King James' book. There were, stated Thomas Potts, two 'degrees of persons' who practised witchcraft: the first were attracted by promises of wealth, and were generally in great poverty, while the second were drawn to the art because of the desire for revenge. In the case of Alice Nutter, this presumed revenge took the form of a conspiracy on her part, along with Elizabeth Device, to bring about the death of one Henry Mitton because of his refusal to give Demdike a penny when she had begged it from him. On the face of it this is a ludicrous accusation, and the only evidence offered by Potts came from James and Jennet Device in their account of the Good Friday meeting at Malkin Tower, a meeting both said was attended by Alice Nutter. Potts also quoted James as saying that the plot to kill Mitton was hatched by Alice and his grandmother, an allegation corroborated by Elizabeth Device, who simply stated that Alice and Demdike 'joined together and bewitched the said Henry Mitton to death'. She added rather enigmatically, that there were two women present at the Good Friday meeting who hailed from Burnley, and that Alice Nutter knew their names.

In all there was nothing new here. The Good Friday meeting had already been much quoted, and with Alice's continuing silence, and very little else to go on, the judge was clearly troubled at the thought of convicting a respectable woman of a capital crime on such meagre evidence. He ordered Thomas Covell to bring the prisoners into court, 'and betwixt every Witch another Prisoner, and some other strange women amongst them, so as no man could judge the one from another'. Having organised what seems to have been one of the first identity parades in English legal history, Bromley had Jennet Device brought into court. The judge 'took great paines to examine her of every particular point'. Who were the people at Malkin Tower? How did she come to know them? How did she know they were witches? Finally Jennet was asked to pick out the person she had accused. A moment whose tension and drama still emerges clearly from the dry mix and jumble of Potts' text was now played out to the court. Jennet Device crossed the space between them and 'went and tooke Alice Nutter by the hand … and told her what place shee sat at the Feast at Malking Tower, at the great assembly of Witches, and who sat next to her: what conference they had, and all the rest of their proceedings at large, without any manner of contrarietie'.

Bromley was still not entirely convinced. He threw a false name at Jennet: 'Johan a Style' (the modern equivalent might be 'Jane Doe'), and asked if that woman was also present, to which Jennet replied that she knew no one of that name. This satisfied the judge, and Potts brought his account to a close by stating that such evidence 'could not be forged or false Accusation, but the very Act of God to discover her'.

Alice was another who refused to admit guilt, even though her own children (and maybe her grandchildren as some commentators put Alice in her fifties, others in her seventies) begged her to repent. She remained silent, 'which was a very fearfull thing to all that were present, who knew shee was guiltie'.

So who was Alice Nutter? Was she what Potts would have us believe – a rich woman who, for reasons of envy or malice, became embroiled in the lives and beliefs and 'devilish practices' of women that were her social inferiors? What motive did she have to do so if this was the case? What had she to envy? Upon whom did she seek revenge, and for what? Why was she at Malkin Tower for the Good Friday meeting – if she actually even was? And why would she take the life of a man for the motive ascribed to her? Was she, as others have suggested, the victim of a plot to do away with her in the hope of personal gain? Conspirators abound in this scenario: all the members of her own family, especially her son Miles, as well as Roger Nowell. Was she a Catholic? If this was the case, was her silence concerning the events of Good Friday 1612 an attempt to protect a priest living clandestinely in the wilds of rural Lancashire?

The reality is that, once again, we really know little enough of her life to allow us to say with any degree of certainty. For example, the myth persists that she was the owner of Roughlee Hall, even though it seems quite clear that this was not the case at all, and that, at best, she was a tenant. There was no evidence that either Alice, or her husband before her, or indeed her son after her, were landowners of any great standing. They were certainly not on a social par with the gentry families of the county. There is no record of a dispute over land with Nowell.

The confusion here seems to have arisen from a mix-up in Alice's very identity. We have already heard that the Robert Nutter whom Anne Whittle was convicted of murdering was the heir to land that contained Chattox's home. She said, in her confession to Nowell, that she had been approached by the boy's own grandmother, Elizabeth Nutter, to kill him so that she would gain control of the property. Unbelievably, there is a story, still in circulation today, which has it that this Elizabeth was in fact Alice, even though they are plainly two different people, and which ignores the fact that Alice was never even charged in connection with that crime. Sadly, such errors become compounded, and take on a life of their own until they become part of the myth, and the myth then morphs into flawed reality.

As to the question of Alice's faith, all we know is that, while there were two priests in her husband's family – one of whom, Robert, was executed for his faith in Lancaster in July 1600 – there is no actual proof that she was a Catholic herself.

Although this is the most satisfactory and enticing theory, once more it is unproven. It would be nice to think that Alice was actually at mass on Good Friday 1612, not at a witches' Sabbat. It would be nice to believe that, faced with the charges of witchcraft, she chose to retain a dignified silence in order to save the life of her priest, even at the cost of her own. Sadly, however, Alice Nutter must remain as enigmatic a figure today as she was nearly four hundred years ago. What we do know for certain is that she stood trial along with the others, that she said nothing in her own defence, and that, notwithstanding her social position or any lingering doubts that might have remained as to her guilt, she was convicted of witchcraft.

The court found her guilty of murdering a man over a penny. If she was the innocent we must believe she was, then it must have seemed to her – alone as she was and reviled as a creature barely human and not deserving of life – that the world had gone mad.

The Trial of Katherine Hewitt

But the madness had yet to run its course. Inexorably the business of the assize moved on to its next victim, and Thomas Potts once again delved into his endless store of hyperbole to bring us the account of the 'evil' that was Katherine Hewitt.

She was, according to Potts, the wife of one John Hewitt, a clothier from Colne. Like Alice Nutter she was unrelated to the Whittles, Devices or Southerns, and it would seem that, with her husband gainfully employed, she too was of a slightly different social class. Potts stated that her nickname – her 'alias' as he put it – was 'Mouldheels', but sadly he did not elaborate on this. Katherine stood accused of the murder of Anne Foulds, to which she pleaded not guilty. Katherine had a co-accused, Alice Grey, but Potts made no mention of her part in the trial. In the finished edition of *The Wonderfull Discoverie*, he listed her as one of the Samlesbury accused, but she then appeared on the list of the people acquitted.

The only evidence against Katherine was that given by Elizabeth Device, her son James and her daughter Jennet. This took the form of yet another rendition of the tale of the Good Friday meeting, with the addition this time of the accusation that, during the gathering, Katherine had admitted, along with one Alice Grey, to having brought about the death of Anne Foulds, the child of one of their neighbours. Both women had also apparently boasted of having another child – that of Michael Hartley, also of Colne – 'in hanck', meaning they were in the process of killing this child as well.

When the time came for Jennet's testimony, the judge once again asked her to pick Katherine out from a line-up, which she did unerringly. As with Alice Nutter, the judge threw a made-up name at the child, who must been a very confident witness indeed, because 'without any manner of contraritie' the child once more played her part to perfection. Amazingly that was all the evidence ever presented against Katherine. The jury was sent out to deliberate on its verdicts, and the morning ended with, as we have seen, the acquittals of the Salmesbury women, and the convictions of Anne Redfearne, Alice Nutter and Katherine Hewitt.

John and Jane Bulcock

John Bulcock and his mother Jane were brought into court on the afternoon of 19 August to answer the charge that they had, by the use of 'Witchcrafts, Inchantments, Charmes and Sorcerie', caused one Jennet Deane to waste and be consumed, after which the said Jennet 'became madde'.

Unusually, Potts began his account by saying that even if there had been nothing more than the evidence that placed the two at the Good Friday meeting, this would have been enough 'to bring their lives to a lawful trial'.

It is important here to look at the terms of the 1604 Act under which all of the defendants in the 1612 trials stood accused. The Act built upon those of Henry VIII and Queen Elizabeth, but under its terms it had become a hanging offence to bring about a death by witchcraft, to invoke spirits, to cause bodily injury, or to steal from graves. If a person were found guilty a second time of divination, administering a love potion or intent to harm, the 'witch' also faced death. This penalty was also prescribed for anyone that aided and abetted in these crimes, and this included anyone who counselled a witch in his or her evil aims. Given that John and Jane had been placed at the Malkin Tower meeting, where the assembly had agreed to help Jennet Preston kill Thomas Lister, and that their own supposed victim had suffered bodily harm at their hands, under the terms of the Act Potts was correctly stating the letter of the law. However, the very fact that he mentioned this at all leads one to wonder if, perhaps with the benefit of hindsight, he was trying to pre-empt and deflect any criticism with regard to this particular trial and its eventual outcome. The Bulcocks also committed the cardinal sin of denying that they had ever been at Malkin Tower and protesting their innocence in a 'very violent and outrageous manner, even to the gallows'.

Since the only evidence against the accused came from Elizabeth Device and her two children, their testimony about the Malkin Tower meeting was duly trotted out yet again. James Device told of hearing the Bulcocks confess to having bewitched Jennet Deane, of Newfield Edge in Yorkshire, so that she would lose her reason. They had also consented to Jennet Preston's supposed plans to kill Thomas Lister. Elizabeth merely stated that she thought John had consented to Lister's murder, and that Jane might know some other witches 'about Padyham and Burnley'. It was left, yet again, to the star witness to cast the killing blow. Jennet once more picked out the accused from a line-up, this time taking the hand of Jane Bulcock. She also recalled seeing John at the Good Friday feast; she remembered him turning the spit on which they were cooking the stolen lamb.

This seems to have been the sum total of the evidence against the two accused. Although in some editions of *The Wonderfull Discoverie* it is stated that the Bulcocks were found not guilty, they were, in fact, condemned and hanged along with the others. But the verdicts had yet to be announced, and before the day's business could be concluded there were three more trials to be completed. The first of these followed immediately, and was that of Alizon Device.

The Trial of Alizon Device

Because, for the first time, Potts had the testimony of the supposed victim to work with, his treatment of Alizon's trial differed somewhat in nature to that of the others. Potts started with a description of John Law: 'a poore distressed pedler', and recounted the history of Alizon's short career as a witch. She had been taught by her grandmother and mother, and had been raised 'in this detestable course of life'. Potts was seemingly supported in this by Alizon herself, who as good as pleaded guilty to the charge of laming Law as soon as she set eyes on her victim.

Law, it appears, had attended all the trials and was then waiting in the 'Moot Hall' outside, ready to give his evidence. He was helped into court by his son, Abraham, and Alizon immediately 'upon her knees at the Barre with weeping teares, prayed the court to hear her'. The judge consented to this and Alizon was allowed to approach the bench where she fell to her knees again and begged forgiveness for her crimes.

She was asked to make a statement, which she duly did, once more telling of her encounters with the 'Blacke-Dogge', as she now described her familiar spirit.

Two years previously, Old Demdike had begun to badger the girl to allow a familiar spirit to approach her as a prelude to becoming a witch. Reluctantly, Alizon had agreed and soon afterwards she had her first encounter with the spirit. He appeared to her on the property of one John Robinson near Roughlee, asked for her soul, and then sucked blood from her breast, leaving behind a blue mark that remained visible for six months. She had not encountered the dog again until he appeared to her on 18 March 1612, immediately prior to her fateful meeting with John Law just outside Colne. Having apparently caused Law to collapse it seems that Alizon followed him to the house where he was being cared for. Seeing what had happened she left to continue begging in Trawden Forest. Five days after this event the Blacke-Dogge once again materialised in front of Alizon near Newchurch, but she refused to speak with him.

Alizon's 'liberall and voluntarie confession' caused some consternation in court, and Judge Bromley immediately asked Law to give his account of the affair. John Law was sworn in and proceeded to give the court his version of what had happened on 18 March 1612. His account varied little from the version already heard. However, he told the court that as he lay in bed in the ale-house to which he had been taken, unable to move either 'hand or foote' he saw 'a great Blacke-Dogge stand by him, with very fearfull firie eyes, great teeth, and a terrible countenance, looking him in the face; whereat he was very sore afraid'. Immediately after this Alizon came into the room, but said nothing and quickly left again. However, Law was 'tormented both day and night with the said Alizon; and so continued lame, not able to travel or take paines ever since that time'.

The drama of the moment must have been intense, especially as, after Law's recounting of how he came to the pitiable state in which he found himself, he turned to Alizon and 'with weeping teares in great passion' he cried to her that she knew this all to be true. Alizon cried out to God to forgive her, once more admitting that she was guilty. She begged John's forgiveness, which, remarkably, 'he very freely and voluntarily' gave, and not for the first time as we have seen. The fact that he had ever given it is all the more surprising when we hear how badly Law had suffered; Potts gave us a graphic account of John Law as he appeared in court that day:

> ... his head is drawne awry, his Eyes and face deformed. His speech not well to be understood; his Thighes and Legges starcke lame; his Armes lame especially the left side, his handes lame and turned out of their course, his Bodie able to endure no travell.

Such was the pity in the court for someone who had been 'a goodly man of stature' before his encounter with Alizon, that she was asked by the judge if she was able to restore him to health. She replied that she could not, but added that Old Demdike, had she lived, would have been able to do so. Alizon, having confessed, was taken away. John Law was told that he too could leave, but not before some of the gentry present – Lord Gerrard and Sir Richard Houghton among them – promised that he would be afforded some 'reliefe and maintenance' at their cost.

The trial appears to have ended at this point, but Potts could not resist removing any shred of sympathy that his readers might still harbour for Alizon Device. He inserted at this juncture a portion of testimony from James Device that described how, being confronted by one Henry Bulcock over her supposed bewitchment of one of his children, Alizon had fallen on her knees and begged forgiveness of him in much the same way she had with John Law. There was a clear implication that

any remorse Alizon might have exhibited in court was feigned, and was all part of her *modus operandi*.

In many respects this case was the pivotal one. It was the incident outside Colne that started the investigations into the Pendle witches to begin with, and without it there are doubts if any of what followed would ever have come to light. It was the last of the trials concerning the two key families, and the only one where a supposed victim was able to give evidence in person. And what a witness John Law proved to be. One can only imagine the tension as Law, aided by his son, was helped into court, as his story unfolded in his own faltering words, as he cried out to Alizon and she in turn admitted her guilt. And perhaps she even believed that she was responsible. While it seems clear that Law suffered a stroke, it did happen to a seemingly healthy man a few moments after Alizon had accepted an offer from the Blacke-Dogge to lame him. According to her testimony, Alizon had resisted the use of witchcraft for a long time, and even Potts admitted that there was some sympathy for her because she was new to the craft.

Given that she was raised amid ignorance and superstition, and that she carried the stigma of belonging to Old Demdike's family, is it possible that she truly believed that she was the cause of John Law's suffering, even perhaps that she was deserving of death for her wickedness. If what she had told Roger Nowell was what she truly believed had happened that day in March, then she must have secretly been astonished when the curse cast upon Law acted so swiftly and terribly, right before her eyes. She followed Law as he was taken into the ale-house, then went to see him as he lay paralysed in bed. If she had brought about this change in him, albeit through her familiar spirit, then what more was she capable of? But if, as we must believe, she had done nothing more than perhaps wish John Law to become ill, and then embroidered upon her guilty feelings once he collapsed, why on earth would she admit to such a thing? It seems probable that all those who stood accused in the 1612 trials were involved to some extent in what might be termed 'the witch business'.

Powerless as they were through ill-health, bereavement and poverty, might they not *want* to believe that they had some vestige of power left to them? They would certainly want their neighbours to believe it, but perhaps, like some progressive illness, that belief had grown and festered until they came to believe in their own propaganda. Without a rational explanation none of the events of 1612 and the years that preceded the trials makes any sense. And for Alizon as for the rest of family, the time was fast approaching when they would pay the ultimate penalty.

The jury retired and when it returned it was to convict John and Jane Bulcock of the indictments against them. Alizon Device was convicted 'upon her owne Confession'.

The Trial of Margaret Pearson

Margaret was the wife of Edward Pearson of Padiham, and this was her third appearance in court on charges relating to witchcraft. On the first occasion she had been accused of murder, on the second of bewitching one of her neighbours, and finally in 1612 she was charged with bringing about the death of one of her neighbour's horses. Margaret's case highlights the fact that an accusation of witchcraft did not mean an automatic conviction. We have already seen that Jennet Preston was acquitted at her first trial in York and, in the trial of Margaret Pearson, we have witnessed the first of the defendants to be spared the death sentence. Thomas Potts was, of course, well aware of the outcome of this trial when he wrote about it, and this was reflected in his tone throughout. He still numbered Margaret among the worst of the witches on trial:

> This wicked and ungodly Witch revenged her furie upon goods, so that every one neare her sustained great lose ... had not the favour and mercie of the Jury beene more than her desert, you [would] have found her next to Old Demdike ...

Of course, this was how Potts saw all the defendants, but there must have been enough doubt, or enough left in them of mercy, for the jury to have saved her. We will, however, never know what it might have been, as Thomas Potts was not of a like mind and was clearly not convinced of her innocence. He was in the business of reporting the conviction of the agents of the Devil, while at the same time lauding his masters, and behind the account of Margaret's trial runs the unmistakable hint of his disapproval at the ultimate verdict.

The evidence was once again slight, although it has to be said no less so than that given against some of the other accused who were later hanged. Margaret was accused of killing one Dodgson's mare, which she did by sitting upon it. There was a common saying in this period that described this – it was known as being 'hag-ridden' and it is from this aspect of witchcraft that we get our modern term 'haggard'. It was used to account for sudden exhaustion and lethargy. Pearson was supposed to have literally tired the mare to death, with, of course, the help of her familiar spirit. Old Chattox had given a description of this familiar to Nowell in April, describing him as a man with cloven hooves. Chattox also told how Margaret confessed to having murdered one Childer's wife and daughter, and also of having bewitched the wife of Mr Pearson of Padiham so that she grew grievously ill.

Evidence was then produced in the form testimony taken by Nicholas Bannister – a fellow JP and associate of Roger Nowell – at Padiham on 9 August. This was supplied by Jennet Booth of Padiham, presumably another of Margaret's neighbours. The account is confusing. First she said that she was at the home of Margaret

Pearson, 'the Friday next after the said Pearson's wife was committed to the Gaole at Lancaster', working in the home carding, so she probably worked for Margaret's husband in some small capacity. She then went on to say that she had 'willed the said Margerie' to give her a little warm milk for the child she had with her. By Margerie did she mean Margaret? This is implied by the language: 'the said Margerie', but if Pearson was already in prison was this an actual encounter or was Jennet merely justifying the taking of the milk to herself? If she is referring to another woman this is never explained or expanded upon. Jennet added wood to the fire, which had burned low in the grate, and set the milk to warm. When she went to remove the pan a 'Toade, or a thing very like a Toade … came out of the fire'. 'Margerie' removed the creature with a pair of tongs and took it out of the house 'but what the said Marjerie did therewith, this Examinate knoweth not'.

This surely implies that Jennet was talking about Margaret, otherwise why was 'Margerie' not in court? And if Margaret was in gaol how could this incident be used as evidence against her? Why was it used at all? Was it perhaps that most rare thing in English witch trials – spectral evidence? This type of evidence was used extensively in America during the Salem Witch Trials, and it involved 'sightings' or 'projections' of a suspected witch, who supposedly appeared to a victim even when they were actually miles away and sometimes in the company of others. Refutation of such evidence was the basis for the acquittals and ultimately the pardons issued in Salem after the trials had been brought to a swift close by the authorities, who were alarmed that people were being sent to the gallows on such flimsy and unsubstantiated evidence. Even though it was never named as spectral evidence in Lancaster in 1612, it is tantalisingly close to being just that according to how Potts presented the evidence. It is also, perhaps of all the testimony heard that summer, perhaps the most ridiculous, and one has to wonder why the court admitted it. Might it be that we are looking at ulterior motives? This evidence was gleaned not by Nowell himself but by Bannister. Was there an element of rivalry between the two JPs-cum-witchhunters? Was Margaret, a woman who was already under suspicion by her neighbours, simply added to the pot, so to speak, in the hope that she would be convicted? Although Old Chattox had given evidence against her did she really know Margaret at all before they had the misfortune to share a gaol cell? As with so much else, all we can do is speculate on the answers to these questions, and wonder at the way such nonsense could be given credence at a time when England was, in many other ways, emerging from a medieval, into a modern world of science and medicine.

Although what was heard in court that late Wednesday afternoon seems to have been sufficient evidence for Thomas Potts, thankfully the jury had believed differently. It is obvious that a toad could easily have been living in the woodpile from which Jennet replenished the fire. It is also obvious that this witness showed herself to be an ingrate. Margaret (if it was she) had been good enough to feed the child of one of her husband's employees and in return had, either from spite or ignorance or some other motive, been accused of a terrible crime.

In the end, although she was to escape the rope, Margaret did not go free. But before her sentence was announced there was one final case to be heard.

Isobel Roby

> Thus at one time may you behold Witches of all sorts from many places in this Countie of Lancaster which now may lawfully bee said to abound as much in Witches of divers kindes as Seminaries, Jesuits and Papists.

Thus Thomas Potts began his account of the final witch trial held in Lancaster that August. Having once more made his point about the inherent and insidious evil of

Catholicism, Potts went on to number the victims – the daughters, sons, kinfolk and friends – snatched from the world by evil. He mentioned by name the work done on the subject by the king himself, and how *Daemonologie* had been vindicated anew by the outcome of the trials at Lancaster. And he noted how, faced with the weight of truth, so many of the accused confessed to their terrible crimes. Last into the dock, and with no direct link to any of the other defendants, was Isobel Roby.

Quite often, when histories of the Lancashire witches are written, Isobel is left as little more than a footnote. There were nine Pendle witches hanged, it is stated … oh, and Isobel Roby, who just happened to be convicted at the same assize. If we are being pedantic there is some truth in this, as Isobel came from Windle, not Pendle, and the evidence against her was not supplied, as in most of the other trials, by any of the Demdike or Chattox clans. Neither had she been brought to trial by Roger Nowell or by Nicholas Bannister, but rather by the hereditary lord of the manor of Windle (near St Helens) – none other than the same Lord Gerrard who had promised relief to John Law. She was, in many respects, an *addendum* to the history of the Pendle Witch Trial. But this is to deny Isobel her place in history, to forget that she appeared before the same judge and was convicted by the same jury. It is to forget that she spent the same amount of time in the dungeon below the Well Tower, or that she went to the moors above the town and died on the same scaffold as her more famous co-defendants. It is to ignore the fact that, as with the Bulcocks, Isobel had not been accused or convicted of taking a human life.

The root cause of the trouble that was finally to bring Isobel before the might of the law, was some feud or difference of opinion between Isobel and the man her god-daughter married, one Peter Chaddock, also of Windle. Isobel had voiced her opposition to the marriage before it took place, whereupon Peter had told her that he didn't care what she thought and that she was probably a witch. He then suffered bouts of severe pain over the next few years, intermittent in nature and on one occasion accompanied by a raging thirst. Others were called to testify, and the by now familiar list of suspicious events, were trotted out in court. On one occasion Jane Wilkinson became ill after refusing Isobel milk; on another Jane felt a sharp pain in her leg as though someone had pinched her. Margaret Lyon told of how Isobel had stated in her presence that Peter Chaddock would never mend until he had apologised to her, a claim borne out by Margaret Parre, who testified that Isobel had admitted to having bewitched both Peter Chaddock and Jane Wilkinson.

It appears that it took very little time for the jury to consider its verdict, and when it returned it was to find Isobel Roby guilty as charged. Thomas Covell was ordered to return all of the accused to court in order that sentence could be passed.

Judgement

There is no man alive more unwilling to pronounce this woefull and heavy Judgement against you, than myselfe: if it were possible, I would to God this cup might passe from me.

Judge Bromley might indeed have been speaking the truth when he said this, but whatever he was feeling he had done the job he was sent to do, and overseen the trials of the people who now stood before him convicted of witchcraft, awaiting only the pronouncement of their fate. The eight women and two men must have already known what that would be, but the words are no less chilling nevertheless. How much worse must it have been to hear them knowing that you were innocent?

But before the sentence was read Bromley was obliged to review the case, a sort of homily designed to reinforce the judgement to come, both in this world and the next:

'What persons of your nature and condition, ever were Arraigned and Tried with more solemnitie, had more libertie given to pleade or answere to everie particular point of Evidence against you?' he asks. 'You have neither cause to be offended in the procedings of the Justices ... nor with the Court that hath had great care to give nothing in evidence against you but matter of fact ... and not to induce the Jurie to finde any one of you guiltie upon matter of suspicion or presumption, nor with the witnesses who have been tired, as it were in the fire ...'

'But the bloud of these innocent children, and others of His Majesties Subjects, whom cruelly and barborously you have murdered, and cut off, with all the rest of your offences, hath cryed out unto the Lord against you, and sollicited for satisfaction and revenge, and that hath brought this heavie judgement upon you at this time ...'

'The worst then I wish to you, standing at the Barre convicted, to receive your Judgement, is Remorse, and true Repentence, for the safeguard of your Soules, and after, an humble, and heartie acknowledgement of your grievous sinnes and offences committed both against God and Man ...'

'Crave pardon of the World, and especially of all such as you have been justly offended, either by tormenting themselves, children, or friends, murder of their kinsfolk, or losse of any of their goods ...'

'It only remains I pronounce the Judgement of the Court against you by the Kings authority which is; You shall all goe from hence to the Castle, from whence you came; from thence you shall be carried to the place of Execution for this Countie where your bodies shall bee hanged untill you be dead; And God Have Mercie Upon Your Soules.'

The judge appointed a preacher for their comfort, and to prepare them for the next world. He told them he would pray for their repentance in this life and forgiveness

for them in the next, and he asked God to grant that they make good use of the time they had left to them, *'to his glorie and your owne comfort'*.

Margaret Pearson was sentenced to stand in the pillories at Lancaster, Clitheroe, Padiham and Whalley on four market days, with a paper on her head upon which was writ large the nature of her offence, and afterwards to remain in prison in Lancaster Castle for one year.

Execution

The place of execution for the county, in 1612, was a spot on the moors above Lancaster, and it was to this place that the condemned would have been conveyed on their final journey from the castle.

A somewhat fanciful tradition states that the witches, en route to their execution and carried through the town in a cart, were allowed to stop at The Golden Lion public house on Moor Lane for a final drink. Although it was certainly used to ease the way to the gallows for those condemned in the nineteenth century, there is sadly no proof that the ale-house existed in 1612, or that the witches were granted this boon at all en route to their deaths. Having said that, this is a quaint-enough tale that gives the modern tourist somewhere tangible to visit in their quest for the witches.

The gallows itself was probably erected on the moor at the top of this road, but its exact site is unknown. What we do know from accounts of other executions in this period is that this would have been a very public and humiliating death. The case was notorious and would have drawn a huge crowd. It is not difficult to imagine the mixture of excitement and hysteria – tinged, no doubt, with just a dash of trepidation – that would have gripped the crowd.

The Pendle witches along with Katherine Hewitt and poor hapless Isobel Roby, would have died on a short drop, a method of execution that continued well into the nineteenth century. Unlike the more humane long drop designed to break the neck, the short drop resulted in a long drawn-out death by strangulation that could take several minutes to achieve its purpose. After the execution the bodies would have remained hanging for up to an hour to ensure that the victims were dead. There are records of people trying to cheat the rope by placing a tube in their throat, indeed there is such a case on the records at the castle. After this it is likely that the bodies would have been burned. But again, we have no record of what happened after execution, and it is just as possible that they were buried, maybe at a crossroads. What we are certain of is that there are no known graves in existence, and that the famous plot at Newchurch-in-Pendle that purports to be the final resting place of Alice Nutter cannot be her grave. Anyone condemned to death was considered anathema, and would not be allowed to lie in the consecrated soil of a churchyard.

And so the last resting place of the witches, as with so much else to do with this case, remains unknown. The court records have been long lost, as have the places mentioned in the trial. Of the main sites quoted only Roughlee Hall still stands, while Nowell's old home at Read Hall was replaced by another house in the eighteenth century. Of Chattox's home, Baldwin's Mill, and of Malkin Tower there is no trace, no matter how many hopefuls theorise that they have 'found' them. Searching through parish registers, the names associated with the case, of both victims and accused, jump from the page. The Pendle area abounds with Nutters and Baldwins, with Pearsons and Dodgsons, and it is possible to catch an echo of the times in the diaries and records of the Gentry families that also played a part in the story and whose lives were better documented.

Epilogue

In Lancaster itself, the home of Thomas Covell still exists in the shape of the old Judges' Lodgings, and of course the castle still dominates the city from its hilltop. But even here there is precious little left that can be directly linked to the trial, beyond the dungeon below the Well Tower. Major improvements at the turn of the nineteenth century swept away the old court where the witches stood trial, once again adding to the sense of elusiveness that seems to surround the case. Demdike and Chattox and their families seem to have slipped through the hands of history. They have certainly taken on a sort of mythic quality, so that it is all too easy, sometimes, to forget that these were real people.

But real they were. The fact of their supposed crimes often blinds us to this fact. The witch is a monster we first encounter in childhood, an eater of babies, a poisoner of princesses, capable of anything from shape-shifting to flying through the night sky astride a broomstick. Each 31 October hordes of children don green makeup and pointed hats – not understanding the symbolism – and cackle their way from door to door 'Trick or Treating'. Many of them, in Lancashire, may even join the crowds that climb Pendle Hill on Hallowe'en, in hope of ... what exactly?

It is absolutely certain that the people condemned at Lancaster Castle in August 1612 would pass unnoticed by any of us – no cauldrons, no broomsticks, very few black cats. They were just, for the most part, either confused or old or sick, or actually believed that they were what the authorities wanted them to be. The Lancashire Witch Trial gave a boost to the careers of the two judges involved, albeit for a brief time in the case of Sir James Altham who died in 1617 aged 62. After his death a contemporary described him as 'one of the gravest and most reverend of the judges of the king' (DNB p. 362).

Sir Edward Bromley was promoted to the more prestigious and lucrative Midland Circuit in 1616 and continued in his career until his death in 1626, aged 63.

Thomas Potts was given a profitable sinecure, being allowed to collect 'the forfeitures on the laws concerning sewers' for a period of 21 years from 1618.

Roger Nowell died of natural causes in 1623.

Thomas Covell died peacefully at his home at the age of 78. He is buried in the Priory Church where his memorial can still be seen.

Justice done, the legal parade left Lancaster later that same month. Over the intervening weeks and months, no doubt the gaol slowly filled again with miscreants awaiting trial in the spring. Potts' book was published in London the following year, and almost from the start the 'Witches of Lancaster' began to exert their pull on the public imagination. Plays, and later on, novels, would assure that they were never forgotten.

The Aftermath

No mention was made of the reaction to the convictions in Lancaster on the part of relatives or friends of the convicted. At the end of his tract Potts did however detail the trial of Jennet Preston in York, which ended in her execution. Here we catch a glimpse of the anguish felt by those left behind when a mother, a daughter or a wife was swept away from them on the tide of fear and superstition that was the witchcraft trial. Potts addressed his remarks primarily to the bereaved family and friends of Jennet Preston, who had obviously been marginally successful in casting doubts about the validity of her conviction and Altham's conduct of her trial:

> You that were husband to this Jennet Preston; her friends and kinsfolke, who have not beene sparing to devise so scandalous a slander out of the malice of your hearts, as that shee was maliciously prosecuted by Master Lister and others (even at the Gallowes where shee died impenitent and void of all feare or grace) she died an Innocent woman, because shee would confesse nothing ...

It is not difficult to guess how Master Preston would have replied to this little rant, and these words allow us a glimpse, albeit second hand, of a very real and very human tragedy. Clearly Preston was in no mood to allow the death of his wife to go unchallenged, even if all he could do was to call the whole proceedings and the verdict into question. He cannot have been alone in his feelings of anger and frustration, but his voice, like so many others, went unheard, and his grief un-assuaged.

And lastly we come to Jennet Device. It is hard to know how she must have felt after almost her entire family had been wiped out. We know that she had at least one uncle, the Christopher Howgate who had had the good sense to flee when he saw which way the wind was blowing. John Clayton raises the interesting possibility that she was taken in and raised by her natural father after the events of 1612. Was she a heroine to her neighbours for having rid the area of the evil they believed themselves to have been victims of, or was she viewed with suspicion, perhaps even quietly reviled for the betrayal of so many members of her family?

For a time Jennet simply disappeared from history. But she was to reappear (or so we believe – certainly a woman of this name was listed among the defendants) at the second of the famous Lancaster trials for witchcraft, in 1634 – like her family twenty-two years previously – accused of being a witch. Clearly, there had never been much hope that she could escape the ghosts of her past. She ultimately faced an accusation of witchcraft and stood trial in the same court as her family and, like them, was found guilty. Ironically the chief evidence against her came from a child, this time a boy, Edmund Robinson. However, times had changed just enough to save Jennet from the same fate to which she had helped consign her family. James I was dead and the new king, James' son Charles, was a more rational, less superstitious man. Learning of the verdicts in Lancashire and having heard of the outlandish claims made against the accused, he ordered a stay of execution until he could himself examine the condemned. Several of Jennet's co-accused made the long journey to London, and the result was acquittal for them all once the boy Edmund and his father were shown to have concocted the whole story in an effort to make themselves rich. Such things took time, however, and there is a tradition in the castle to this day that, in all, Jennet Device spent three years incarcerated there. One can only wonder if the ghosts of her past ever manifested themselves to her as she sat in the same darkness from which her grandmother, mother, brother and sister were never to emerge alive.

Conclusion

The trials at Lancaster in August 1612 are among the most famous cases of witchcraft in English history. For most of the remainder of the seventeenth century sporadic outbreaks of witchcraft accusations were to plunge whole areas of the country into terror, and thanks to the wonderful and painstaking research into the subject by notable social historians today we are able to read about many of them in great detail, and to catch a glimpse of the society, and the complexities of belief, fear and anxiety that lay behind an accusation of witchcraft. We have also, hopefully, come to a better understanding of the social pressures, the religious turmoil and the economic factors that all played a part in such accusations. By 1683 the last witch to die in England at the hands of the law had gone to the gallows, and as we have noted, by the middle of the following century the very idea that such a being could exist was being scoffed at – at least in elite circles.

Other countries suffered their own outbreaks, heard more hysterical children tell tales of the impossible, and sent more men and women into the flames or to the rope's end. One of the most notorious trials of all took place in Salem, Massachusetts, in 1692, and there is a very human connection with the events in America and those that took place in Lancaster eighty years before (over and above the fact that the Pendle case was referenced in a magistrates' handbook that would have been in use in the colonies at this time, and which cites Jennet Device's evidence as a model for the use of child witnesses in witchcraft trials). The respected Puritan Divine, Cotton Mather was brought in as a consultant to the judges in the Salem trials. Mather's grandfather had been born in Lancashire, and the trials at Lancaster had obviously left an indelible mark on him. He had passed on his experiences to his family, so much so that his grandson was to equate the events of 1612 to what was happening in Massachusetts. The Salem case was different in many respects to the events in Lancashire, but the outcome was chillingly similar. And although not directly responsible for the many executions that followed the Salem trials, it is interesting to see how ideas and memories can shape the way the world operates, even over thousands of miles, and many, many years.

It is interesting to note that the last prosecution in England for a witchcraft-related death came in 1751 with the execution of one John Colley in Hertfordshire. But John was not a suspected witch. Rather, he was hanged for leading a mob that attacked an old woman, Ruth Osborne, and murdered her by 'swimming' her in the local pond. Osborne has long been suspected of being a witch, and her neighbours had finally taken the law into their own hands. At the time, not quite 150 years after the Pendle Trials, it was clear to the elite that such beliefs were the result of foolishness and ignorance. It also seems clear that at grass-roots levels such beliefs were very much alive, and that women such as Ruth Osborne were still seen as the instruments of evil in exactly the same way that Demdike and the others had been seen so long before. But as this book has concentrated so heavily upon him, perhaps the last words should belong to Thomas Potts:

Looke not upon things strangely alledged, but judiciously consider what is justly proved against them ...

The wheel of history has turned, and it seems clear that the trials in Lancaster Castle in August 1612 had very little in them of justice, and nothing at all that would stand today as proof. I am certain that Thomas Potts would be amazed that his words could ever be used to hint at the innocence of the men and women of whose guilt he was, all those years ago, so frighteningly certain.

The Witches and their Victims: the sixteen deaths attributed to the defendants in the 1612 trials.

Old Demdike (Died before trial)

Richard Assheton
The Child of Richard Baldwin
Henry Mitton

Old Chattox

Robert Nutter
John Device
Anne Nutter
John Moore
Hugh Moore

Katherine Hewitt

Anne Foulds

Elizabeth Device

John Robinson
James Robinson
Henry Mitton

James Device

Anne Towneley
John Hargreaves
Blaze Hargreaves
John Duckworth

Anne Redfearne

Christopher Nutter

Appendix One

Witchcraft — Marks & Tests

Interestingly the discovery of a witch and the tests used to prove or disprove the validity of an accusation that were still extant within popular culture actually had their roots in the Middle Ages, when trials meant just that: the accused underwent a ritual that left it to God to decide guilt or innocence.

The most famous of these tests were the 'pricking' and 'swimming' of a suspected witch. In the former, a needle was inserted into any unusual mark on the suspect's body. These marks ranged from a third nipple to a birthmark, and were commonly believed to indicate the place where the Devil sucked the witch's blood, the area being supposedly impervious to pain. Both Demdike and Chattox told of this taking place at the beginning of their 'careers' as witches. Pricking was a method much favoured by the notorious Matthew Hopkins, the self-styled Witchfinder General who was at work in East Anglia during the Civil War. Paid by the head, he found witches aplenty, and when he was finally revealed as a fraud, a needle was discovered among his possessions which had been used on numerous suspects. It contained a retractable point, so that although to a casual observer it looked as though the needle – when applied to a suspect's body – was entering the flesh, in fact it was sliding back into its housing. The victim, blindfolded, obviously felt nothing, and those called upon to witness the test were presented with seemingly irrefutable evidence of guilt.

'Swimming' involved tying the suspect hand and foot and then throwing them into a pond or river. If the water accepted the accused it was seen as a second baptism and the person was deemed innocent, although sadly by this time most would have already drowned. If the suspect floated then the water had rejected them – they were clearly guilty – at which point they were usually taken out and hanged.

Although the use of torture was not strictly permitted under English law for anything other than treason, these tests came perilously close to being just that. Given that the suspects were usually old or ill-educated with no one to speak for them, it is easy to see how convincing the tests could seem to on-lookers already in a state of fear and apprehension. Witchcraft struck at the heart of a society; the loss of a loved one, of crops or cattle could spell ruin. And anyone could be the witch's next victim. Testing like this gave a gloss of validity, a veneer of legality. While there is no suggestion that such methods were ever used against the suspects of 1612 – perhaps, as we have seen, with the exception of James Device – it is impossible to be certain, and something as simple as sleep-deprivation could produce a confession if it went on long enough.

Appendix Two

The Witches' Tower

The Well Tower lies on the eastern side of Lancaster Castle. It is flanked today by later additions to the castle in the form of the Governor's House (1788) and the Male Felons Tower (1796), but the Well Tower itself is believed to date from the early years of the fourteenth century.

The stonework of this tower differs subtly in colour from the rest of building, indicating that it belongs to a much earlier period (possibly fourteenth century), and the tower has just three small windows visible from the outside, although more can be seen that have been bricked over. Of all the towers in the castle this is probably the least used, and therefore the least altered. An archaeological survey carried out in the early 1990s by Lancaster University mapped each stone and staircase, and interestingly revealed, bricked into one of the walls, a pair of shoes. They have been dated to the eighteenth century, but their position is significant: shoes, as well as other everyday objects, were often bricked up in stairs and chimneys as protection against witchcraft.

Even today, the dungeon below the Well Tower is an evocative place. It is reached through the courtyard of what was, until March 2011, a category C prison, and as the thick wooden door is opened it reveals a steep flight of stone steps dropping away down into darkness. To the left of the door is one of the many wells that dot the hilltop. Rain from the roof of the tower still finds its way there, and the lichen-covered walls of the well echo to the sound of steadily dripping water. There is no electricity in the tower, and the descent to the cell at the base of the steps, some twenty-five feet in total, is made by torchlight. The shifting shadows reveal, at the bottom and to the right, the cell where the Pendle and Samlesbury accused spent what must have been a terrible few months awaiting trial throughout the summer of 1612. The ceiling and walls of the cell are covered with wattle and daub. It has a stone floor set with two metal rings. Tradition has it that the people held in the dungeon over that summer were shackled to the floor, and such traditions should not be lightly disregarded. We know that the dungeon was still used – albeit as a last resort and only on the most intransigent and violent prisoners – as a punishment cell in the last years of the eighteenth century, and there is no evidence to suggest that it had been touched over the intervening years.

The Witchcraft Acts

Witchcraft Act 1541

This was the first Act to class witchcraft as a felony – something that could be tried in a criminal rather than an ecclesiastic court. This meant of course that harsher penalties, including death, could be imposed for crimes such as the divination of treasure in addition to causing harm by magical means. The Act was repealed during the reign of Edward VI in 1547.

Witchcraft Act 1562

Queen Elizabeth I came to the throne following the death of her sister Mary and many of Elizabeth's religious advisors returned to England during this time having fled the country in fear of their lives under her sister's ultra-Catholic regime. It is quite likely that the tone of the legislation reflected their knowledge of what was happening on the continent. The Act called for the death penalty for anyone who had caused death by magical means, while lesser transgressions were more leniently dealt with.

Scottish Witchcraft Act 1563

Often overlooked in the history of English cases, this was a vital piece of legislation, given that King James VI of Scotland ascended the English throne just nine years before the trials in Lancaster. Under the terms of the Act those who practised witchcraft and those who consulted with them were guilty of a capital offence.

Witchcraft Act 1604

This was the Act in force when the Lancashire witches were tried. It became law within a year of James' accession and was harsher than that enacted under Elizabeth. It made causing harm – even that which did not lead to death – a capital crime. In addition it decreed death for anyone found guilty of committing a second punishable offence. It also proscribed the use of dead bodies in magic or the keeping (as opposed to the conjuration) of spirits. In effect it made it much simpler to convict a suspect, as the burden of proof was much reduced.

Witchcraft Act 1735

This Act was an attempt to restrict the number of people claiming to possess magical powers rather than an act against the practice of the craft for evil purposes. It targeted anyone claiming to be able to tell fortunes, cast spells or divine hidden treasure; anyone who did so was, by this time, believed to be a fraud. In effect it passed into law the concept that there was no such thing as a witch, only fraudsters trying to extort money from the gullible. Anyone convicted faced fines and imprisonment. It remained in force until 1951 when it was replaced by The Fraudulent Mediums Act.

Interestingly, an attempt to quash the convictions handed down in Lancaster in August 1612 was denied in 1998 by the then Home Secretary, Jack Straw.

Further Reading

Baines, Edward, *The History of the County Palatine of Lancaster*, Vol. 1 and Vol. 2 (Fisher, Son & Co.: London, 1836)

Barry, Jonathan (ed), *Witchcraft in Early Modern Europe: Studies in Culture and Belief* (Cambridge University Press: Cambridge, 1996)

Bossy, John, *The English Catholic Community 1570–1850* (Darton, Longman, Todd: London, 1975)

Briggs, R., *Witches and neighbours: The social and Cultural Context of European Witchcraft* (Harper Collins: London, 1993)

Clayton, John A.,*The Lancashire Witch Conspiracy: A History of Pendle Forest and the Pendle Witch Trials* (Barrowford Press: East Lancashire, 2007)

Cohn, Norman, *Europe's Inner Demons* (Pimlico: London, 1993)

Coward, Barry, *The Stuart Age, England 1603–1714* (Longman: London, 1980)

Oxford Dictionary of National Biography, (Smith, Elder & Co.: London, 1885-1900)

Francis, Richard, *Judge Sewell's Apology: The Salem Witch Trials and the Forming of a Conscience* (Harper: London, 2006)

Gaskell, Malcolm, *Witchfinders: A Seventeenth Century English Tragedy* (John Murray: London, 2005)

Gibson, Marion (ed), *Witchcraft and Society in England and America 1550–1750* (Cornell University Press: Ithaca, 2003)

Hasted, Rachel A.C., *The Pendle Witch Trial 1612* (Lancashire County Books: Lancashire, 1993)

Hutton, Ronald, *Triumph of the Moon* (Oxford Paperbacks: Oxford, 1995)

Levack, Brian P., *The Witch-Hunt in Early Modern Europe* (Longman: London, 1987)

Lumby, Jonathan, *The Lancashire Witch Craze: Jennet Preston and the Lancashire Witches 1612* (Carnegie: Lancaster, 1995)

MacFarlane, Alan, *Witchcraft in Tudor and Stuart England* (Routledge: Oxon, 1970)

Moorehouse, Geoffrey, *The Pilgrimage of Grace* (Weidenfeld and Nicolson: London, 2002)

Notestein, Wallace, *A History of Witchcraft in England from 1558–1718* (The American Historical Association: Washington, 1911)

Peel, Edgar and Southern, Pat, *The Trials of the Lancashire Witches* (Hendon: Lancashire, 1994)

Poole, R. (ed), *The Lancashire Witches: Histories and Stories* (Manchester University Press: Manchester, 2002)

Potts, Thomas, *The Wonderfull Discoverie of Witches in the Countie of Lancaster* (London, 1613)

Quaife, G.R., *Godly Zeal and Furious Rage: The Witch Hunt in Early Modern England* (Croome Helm: London, 1987)

Scot, Reginald, *The Discoverie of Witchcraft* (London, 1584)

Sharpe, James, *Instruments of Darkness: Witchcraft in Early Modern England* (University of Pennsylvania Press: Pennsylvania, 1997)

Sprenger, J. and Kramer, H., *Malleus Maleficarum 1489* (Various editions)

Thomas, Keith, *Religion and the Decline of Magic* (Penguin: London, 1971)

Thurston, Robert W., *Witch, Wicce, Mother Goose* (Longman: London, 2001)

Also:

Ainsworth, W. Harrison *The Lancashire Witches* (Routledge: Oxon, 1884)

Mulholland, Kate, *A Cry of Innocence* (Devereux Publishing: Lancashire, 2006)

Mulholland, Kate, *The Icarus Legacy* (Devereux Publishing: Lancashire, 2008)

Neill, Robert, *Mist Over Pendle* (Hutchinson: London, 1951)